MAKE THIS YEAR YOUR BEST YEAR

INVESTING 101: A BEGINNER'S GUIDE TO BUILDING WEALTH

Investing 101: A Beginner's Guide to Building Wealth

Investing 101: A Beginner's Guide to Building Wealth

Investing 101: A Beginner's Guide to Building Wealth

Trient Press
3375 S Rainbow Blvd
#81710, SMB 13135
Las Vegas,NV 89180

Ordering Information:
Quantity sales. Special discounts are available on quantity purchases by corporations, associations, and others. For details, contact the publisher at the address above.
Orders by U.S. trade bookstores and wholesalers. Please contact Trient Press: Tel: (775) 996-3844; or visit www.trientpress.com.

Printed in the United States of America

Publisher's Cataloging-in-Publication data
Ruscsak, M.L.
A title of a book :Working for Your Dreams: Investing 101: A Beginner's Guide to Building Wealth
ISBN
Paperback   978-1-955198-09-7
E-book   978-1-955198-08-0

Investing is a crucial part of financial planning and can help you achieve your financial goals. It's important to understand the different types of investments and how they work, so you can make informed decisions about where to put your money.

Stocks are one of the most popular forms of investment, and for good reason. When you buy stocks, you're buying a small piece of ownership in a company. If the company performs well, the value of your stocks can increase, which means you can sell them for more than you paid. Of course, the opposite is also true - if the company performs poorly, the value of your stocks can decrease.

Web3 is a newer form of investment that's gaining popularity. It's a term used to describe the next evolution of the internet, which will be decentralized and powered by blockchain technology. There are many ways to invest in web3, such as buying cryptocurrencies like Bitcoin or investing in decentralized finance (DeFi) projects.

Real estate is another popular investment option. When you buy real estate, you're buying a physical property like a house or a commercial building. Real estate can provide a steady stream of income through rent payments, and the value of the property can increase over time.

These are just a few examples of the different types of investments you can make. It's important to do your research and understand the risks and potential rewards of each type of investment. Remember, investing always comes with some level of risk, so it's important to only invest what you can afford to lose.

Investing 101: A Beginner's Guide to Building Wealth

CHAPTER 1 - A BRIEF HISTORY OF STOCKS

❖ What Are Stocks?
❖ How Do Stocks Work?
❖ Types of Stock
❖ Factors That Affect Stock Prices
❖ Risks and Benefits of Investing in Stocks
❖ Stocks Vs Other Forms of Investment

Introduction

Stocks are a popular investment vehicle that can provide the opportunity for both short-term gains and long-term growth. But before you can start investing in stocks, it's important to have a basic understanding of what they are, how they work, and the potential risks and benefits involved.

The purpose of this chapter is to provide an overview of stocks, and why understanding them is important for anyone interested in investing. We'll start by defining what stocks are, and explain how they work within the context of publicly traded companies. Then, we'll explore why companies offer stocks to the public, and how they can be bought and sold on stock exchanges. We'll also examine some of the factors that can impact stock prices, as well as the potential risks and benefits of investing in stocks.

Whether you're a beginner or an experienced investor, this chapter will give you a solid foundation for understanding stocks, and help you make informed decisions about your investment portfolio. So, let's get started!

What Are Stocks?

Section 1: Definition of stocks

Stocks are ownership shares in a publicly-traded company. When you buy stocks, you become a part-owner of the company and have a claim on its assets and earnings. The more stocks you own, the larger your ownership stake in the company.

Section 2: Owning stocks as an investment

Owning stocks can provide a way to invest in a company and potentially earn a return on your investment. When a company does well, its earnings and assets grow, and its stock price often goes up as well. This means that if you own stocks in the company, the value of your investment can also go up. If the company pays out dividends, which are a portion of its profits to shareholders, you may also receive a regular income from your investment.

However, it's important to keep in mind that investing in stocks comes with risks. The stock market can be unpredictable, and stock prices can fluctuate based on a variety of factors such as economic conditions, company performance, and investor sentiment. It's important to do your research and understand the risks involved before investing in any stock.

Why Do Companies Offer Stocks?

If you're considering investing in the stock market, you may have wondered why companies offer stocks in the first place. It can be confusing to think about why a company would want to give away a portion of its ownership to outside investors. In this chapter, we'll explore the reasons behind why companies offer stocks and how it can benefit both the company and its shareholders.

Overview of Why Companies Offer Stocks

First, let's discuss what we mean by "offering stocks." When a company decides to offer stocks to the public, it's essentially selling a portion of its ownership to outside investors. These investors become shareholders in the company, and they have the potential to earn returns on their investment through dividends or increases in the stock's price.

But why would a company want to give up a portion of its ownership to outside investors? One reason is to raise capital. When a company needs funding for operations or growth, it can turn to the public markets to raise money by offering stocks. By selling shares to investors, the company can raise the capital it needs without taking on debt or giving up control to a single investor.

Another reason a company might offer stocks is to provide liquidity for its existing shareholders. When a company is privately owned, it can be difficult for its owners to sell their shares. By going public and offering stocks on a public exchange, the company's owners can sell their shares more easily, providing them with a way to exit their investment or access additional capital.

Finally, offering stocks to the public can help raise the company's profile and increase its visibility. Public companies are required to disclose financial information to the public, which can attract new investors and help raise awareness of the company's products and services.

How Issuing Stocks Can Provide Capital for Companies

Now let's dive deeper into the primary reason companies offer stocks: to raise capital. When a company offers stocks to the public, it's essentially selling ownership in the company to outside investors. These investors are willing to buy the stocks because they believe that the company will use the funds raised to grow and generate profits.

There are two primary ways a company can raise capital by issuing stocks: through an initial public offering (IPO) or a secondary offering.

An IPO is when a company first goes public and offers stocks for the first time. The company typically hires an investment bank to manage the IPO process and help determine the initial stock price. The investment bank will then market the stock to potential investors and underwrite the offering.

When the IPO is complete, the company receives the proceeds from the sale of the stocks. It can then use this capital to fund its operations, invest in new products or services, pay off debt, or make acquisitions.

A secondary offering is when a company issues additional stocks after its IPO. This can be done for a variety of reasons, such as funding new projects or acquisitions or paying off debt. In a secondary offering, existing shareholders may also have the opportunity to sell their shares in the company.

Overall, issuing stocks can provide companies with a way to raise capital without taking on debt or giving up control to a single investor. By selling ownership in the company to a large number of investors, the company can access the capital it needs to grow and expand its operations.

Conclusion

In summary, companies offer stocks to the public to raise capital, provide liquidity for existing shareholders, and increase the company's visibility. By issuing stocks, a company can raise capital without taking on debt or giving up control to a single investor. This can provide a win-win situation for both the company and its shareholders, as investors have the potential to earn returns on their investment while the company has the capital it needs to fund its operations and growth.

How Do Stocks Work?

Stocks represent a form of ownership in a publicly-traded company. As a shareholder, you are a part-owner of the company, and have the right to vote on certain matters related to the business, as well as the potential to earn a return on your investment.

But how do stocks actually work? How do you buy and sell them, and what are the different types of stocks available? In this chapter, we'll explore the mechanics of buying and selling stocks on stock exchanges, as well as the different types of stocks and their characteristics.

Mechanics of Buying and Selling Stocks

When you want to buy or sell a stock, you typically do so through a brokerage firm. A brokerage is a financial institution that acts as an intermediary between buyers and sellers of securities, such as stocks, bonds, and mutual funds.

To buy a stock, you first need to open a brokerage account and deposit funds into it. You can then place an order to buy a specific stock at a certain price, which is executed by your broker. The price of a stock is determined by supply and demand in the market, so it can fluctuate constantly throughout the day.

When you buy a stock, you become a shareholder in the company, which means you own a portion of the company's assets and profits. As a shareholder, you are entitled to a portion of any dividends the company may pay, as well as the potential for capital gains if the stock price increases.

When you sell a stock, you receive the proceeds of the sale, which can either be reinvested in other stocks or withdrawn from your brokerage account.

Types of Stocks

There are two main types of stocks: common and preferred.

Common stock is the most common type of stock, and represents ownership in the company with voting rights on certain matters, such as electing board members and approving major company decisions. Common stockholders are also entitled to a portion of the company's profits, but dividends are not guaranteed and are typically paid out after preferred dividends are paid.

Preferred stock, on the other hand, represents ownership in the company with priority on dividends and distributions of assets in the event of a company liquidation. Preferred stockholders do not have voting rights, but are typically entitled to a fixed dividend payment that is paid before any dividends are paid to common stockholders.

In addition to common and preferred stock, there are also other types of stock, such as dual-class stock and convertible stock. Dual-class stock is a type of common stock that gives certain shareholders more voting rights than others, while convertible stock can be converted into a different type of security, such as common stock or bonds, at a predetermined price and date.

Conclusion

Stocks are an important investment vehicle for individuals and companies alike, and understanding how they work is key to making informed investment decisions. By buying and selling stocks, you can become a part-owner of a publicly-traded company and potentially earn a return on your investment. And by understanding the different types of stocks and their characteristics, you can make more informed investment decisions that align with your financial goals and risk tolerance.

Factors That Affect Stock Prices

When investing in stocks, it's important to understand the factors that affect stock prices. Many different factors can influence the stock market, some of which are more predictable than others. Here are some of the main factors to consider:

Company performance: The financial performance of the company is often the most important factor that affects the stock price. If a company is generating strong earnings and revenue growth, investors are more likely to buy the stock, which can drive up the price. On the other hand, if a company is experiencing declining earnings or revenue, investors may be less likely to invest in the stock, which can lead to a drop in the stock price.

Economic conditions: Economic conditions can have a significant impact on the stock market. When the economy is strong, companies tend to perform well, which can lead to higher stock prices. Conversely, when the economy is weak, companies may struggle, and stock prices may decline. Factors that can impact the economy include inflation, interest rates, and economic indicators such as GDP and consumer confidence.

Industry trends: Industry trends can also affect the stock market. For example, if there is a new technology that is disrupting an industry, companies that are slow to adapt may see their stock prices decline. Conversely, companies that are at the forefront of new trends may see their stock prices rise.

Political factors: Political events can have a significant impact on the stock market. For example, changes in government policy, international trade agreements, or geopolitical events can all affect investor sentiment and impact stock prices.

Market sentiment: Market sentiment refers to the overall attitude of investors toward the market. If investors are optimistic, they are more likely to buy stocks, which can drive up prices. Conversely, if investors are pessimistic, they may be more likely to sell stocks, which can lead to a decline in prices.

Supply and demand: Finally, supply and demand also play a role in the stock market. If there are more buyers than sellers, the stock price will go up. Conversely, if there are more sellers than buyers, the stock price will go down.

It's important to remember that these factors are all interconnected, and that changes in one area can impact the others. For example, if there is a recession, companies may struggle, which can lead to a decline in the stock market. Similarly, if there is a major political event, investor sentiment may shift, which can impact the overall demand for stocks.

In summary, there are many different factors that can affect stock prices, and investors need to be aware of these factors when making investment decisions. By understanding the various factors that influence the stock market, investors can make more informed investment decisions and better manage their risk.

Risks and Benefits of Investing in Stocks

When it comes to investing, there are many different options available, but one of the most popular and well-known is investing in stocks. Stocks can offer the potential for high returns, but also come with certain risks that investors need to be aware of. In this chapter, we'll explore the risks and benefits of investing in stocks, and discuss the importance of diversification and long-term investing.

First, let's start with the potential benefits of investing in stocks. One of the biggest benefits is the potential for high returns. Over the long term, stocks have historically offered higher returns than many other types of investments, such as bonds or savings accounts. This is because stocks represent ownership in a company, and as the company grows and becomes more profitable, the value of its shares can increase.

Another benefit of investing in stocks is that they offer the potential for dividend payments. When a company makes a profit, it can choose to pay a portion of those profits to its shareholders in the form of dividends. These payments can provide investors with a steady stream of income, which can be especially appealing for those who are retired or looking for a way to supplement their other sources of income.

However, there are also risks associated with investing in stocks that investors need to be aware of. One of the biggest risks is the possibility of losses. Unlike savings accounts or bonds, stocks do not offer a guaranteed rate of return. In fact, the value of stocks can fluctuate widely from day to day or even minute to minute. If you need to sell your stocks during a period of decline, you could end up losing money.

Another risk of investing in stocks is the possibility of volatility. Stocks can be affected by a wide variety of factors, including economic conditions, changes in the company's management or leadership, and even unexpected events such as natural disasters or pandemics. This volatility can be unsettling for some investors, and can lead to emotional decision-making that can negatively impact their investment performance.

So how can investors mitigate these risks? One important strategy is diversification. By investing in a variety of different stocks and other types of assets, such as bonds or real estate, investors can spread their risk and potentially reduce the impact of any individual stock's performance on their overall portfolio. Another strategy is to take a long-term view of investing. Historically, stocks have performed well over the long term, but short-term fluctuations are a normal part of the investment process.

In summary, investing in stocks can offer the potential for high returns and dividend payments, but also comes with certain risks, including the possibility of losses and volatility. To mitigate these risks, investors should consider diversification and take a long-term view of investing. By doing so, investors can potentially reap the benefits of stock investing while minimizing their exposure to potential risks.

Reminder of the importance of understanding stocks before investing in them

How Stocks Can Help You Build Wealth

Investing in stocks can be a powerful tool for building wealth. Historically, stocks have provided higher returns than many other investment options, including savings accounts, bonds, and real estate. While investing in stocks carries some risk, there are strategies you can use to mitigate that risk and increase your chances of success.

In this chapter, we'll explore the benefits of investing in stocks, the risks involved, and the strategies you can use to build wealth through stock investments.

The Benefits of Investing in Stocks

One of the biggest benefits of investing in stocks is the potential for high returns. While the stock market can be volatile in the short term, over the long term it has historically provided higher returns than other types of investments. For example, according to data from the S&P 500, the average annual return for the stock market between 1926 and 2019 was 10%.

Another benefit of investing in stocks is the ability to generate passive income through dividends. Many companies pay dividends to their shareholders, which can provide a steady stream of income. Dividends are typically paid quarterly, although some companies pay them monthly or annually. While not all stocks pay dividends, those that do can be an attractive option for income investors.

In addition to the potential for high returns and passive income, investing in stocks provides an opportunity to participate in the growth of successful companies. When you buy a stock, you become a part owner of that company. As the company grows and becomes more profitable, the value of your shares can increase, providing a capital gain.

The Risks of Investing in Stocks

While investing in stocks has the potential to provide high returns, it also carries some risk. The stock market can be volatile, and stock prices can fluctuate based on a variety of factors, including economic conditions, company performance, and investor sentiment. It's important to understand that there is always a risk of losing money when investing in stocks.

Another risk of investing in stocks is the potential for fraud. Unfortunately, there are scams and fraudulent schemes in the stock market, so it's important to do your due diligence and research any company before investing in it. Make sure the company is legitimate, financially stable, and has a solid business plan.

Strategies for Building Wealth Through Stock Investments

To mitigate the risks of investing in stocks and increase your chances of success, there are several strategies you can use. One of the most important is diversification. Diversification means spreading your investments across different types of stocks, sectors, and asset classes. This helps to reduce your overall risk, as losses in one area can be offset by gains in another.

Another important strategy is to invest for the long term. While the stock market can be volatile in the short term, over the long term it has historically provided higher returns than other types of investments. By investing for the long term, you can ride out short-term fluctuations and take advantage of the long-term growth potential of the stock market.

It's also important to do your research and choose stocks that are appropriate for your investment goals and risk tolerance. There are many different types of stocks, including growth stocks, value stocks, and dividend stocks. Each type of stock has its own characteristics and risks, so it's important to choose stocks that align with your investment strategy.

Conclusion

Investing in stocks can be a powerful tool for building wealth over the long term. While there are risks involved, there are also many benefits, including the potential for high returns, passive income through dividends, and the opportunity to participate in the growth of successful companies. By using strategies such as diversification, long-term investing, and careful stock selection, you can mitigate the risks and increase your chances of success in the stock market.

Stocks Vs Other Forms of Investment

Investing is a great way to grow your wealth over time. With so many investment options available, it can be difficult to decide where to put your money. Two of the most popular forms of investment are stocks and other assets, such as bonds, real estate, and commodities. In this chapter, we'll explore the differences between stocks and other forms of investment, and help you decide which one might be right for you.

Stocks

A stock is a type of security that represents ownership in a company. When you buy a share of stock, you become a part owner of that company. As a shareholder, you are entitled to a portion of the company's profits and may receive a dividend if the company pays one. In addition, you can sell your shares on a stock exchange if you want to realize a profit or cut your losses.

One of the main benefits of investing in stocks is the potential for high returns. Stocks have historically outperformed other forms of investment over the long term. However, stocks can also be volatile, and their value can fluctuate wildly over short periods of time. As a result, investing in stocks requires a long-term perspective and a willingness to ride out short-term market fluctuations.

Other Forms of Investment

There are many other forms of investment that you may consider, including:

Bonds - Bonds are a type of debt security that represents a loan made by an investor to a company or government. In exchange for the loan, the company or government agrees to pay the investor a fixed interest rate over a specified period of time. Bonds are generally considered to be less risky than stocks, but they also offer lower returns.

Real Estate - Real estate investment can take many forms, from owning rental properties to investing in real estate investment trusts (REITs). Real estate can provide a steady income stream and may offer the potential for long-term capital appreciation. However, real estate investment also requires a significant up-front investment and may involve a high level of risk.

Commodities - Commodities are physical goods that are traded on markets, such as gold, oil, and agricultural products. Commodity prices are subject to supply and demand, and may be affected by global economic conditions. Investing in commodities can provide diversification to a portfolio, but may also be subject to significant price fluctuations.

Which is Right for You?

Deciding which type of investment is right for you depends on your individual circumstances and investment goals. If you're looking for high returns and are willing to accept some risk, stocks may be a good option. However, if you're looking for a more stable income stream, bonds or real estate may be a better fit. Commodities may be a good option for diversification, but they can also be volatile and subject to significant price fluctuations.

It's important to remember that investing always involves some degree of risk, and no investment is a sure thing. It's important to do your research and carefully consider your investment goals and risk tolerance before making any investment decisions. Working with a financial advisor can also be helpful in creating an investment plan that is tailored to your individual needs and goals.

Conclusion

Stocks and other forms of investment can provide opportunities for growth and income, but they each come with their own risks and benefits. Understanding the differences between stocks and other forms of investment is an important first step in creating an investment plan that is right for you. With the right investment strategy, you can build wealth and achieve your financial goals over the long term.

Investing 101: A Beginner's Guide to Building Wealth

CHAPTER 2 - TYPES OF STOCKS

Now that we have covered the basics of what stocks are and how they work, it's time to dive deeper into the different types of stocks available for investors to consider. Understanding the various types of stocks is important for building a well-diversified portfolio that aligns with your investment goals and risk tolerance.

In this chapter, we will explore the different types of stocks that are available, including common and preferred stocks, as well as the features and characteristics of each. By the end of this chapter, you will have a clearer understanding of the types of stocks that are available and be better equipped to make informed investment decisions.

When it comes to investing in stocks, there are several different types of stocks to consider. Each type of stock has its own unique characteristics, advantages, and risks. In this chapter, we will explore the most common types of stocks and what you need to know before investing in them.

Common Stocks:

Common stocks are the most common type of stock and are also known as ordinary shares. When you invest in common stocks, you are buying a share of ownership in a company. Common stocks represent a claim on a company's assets and earnings, and give investors the right to vote on certain corporate decisions, such as the election of the board of directors.

Common stocks are considered a growth investment because their value can appreciate over time. However, common stocks are also considered more volatile than other types of stocks, and their value can fluctuate dramatically in response to market conditions, company performance, and other factors.

Preferred Stocks:

Preferred stocks are a type of stock that gives investors a priority claim on a company's assets and earnings. Preferred stockholders receive dividends before common stockholders, and in the event of bankruptcy, preferred stockholders have a higher priority in the distribution of assets.

Preferred stocks are less volatile than common stocks and are considered a more stable investment. However, they also offer lower potential returns than common stocks. Preferred stocks can also have a fixed dividend rate, meaning that the dividend payment is the same every quarter or year.

Blue Chip Stocks:

Blue chip stocks are shares in large, well-established companies with a history of stable earnings and dividends. These companies are usually industry leaders and are known for their high-quality products, services, and management. Blue chip stocks are considered a conservative investment and are often favored by long-term investors who are looking for a reliable stream of income and stable growth.

Because blue chip stocks are well-established and have a history of success, they are often less volatile than other types of stocks. However, they may also offer lower potential returns than other types of stocks, and their growth potential may be limited.

Growth Stocks:

Growth stocks are shares in companies that are expected to grow at a faster rate than the overall market. These companies are often in emerging industries or have innovative products or services. Growth stocks are considered a higher risk, higher potential reward investment.

Growth stocks can be volatile, and their value can fluctuate dramatically based on company performance, market conditions, and other factors. However, if the company succeeds, growth stocks can offer significant potential returns.

Value Stocks:

Value stocks are shares in companies that are considered undervalued by the market. These companies may have a strong balance sheet, stable earnings, and other positive characteristics, but their stock price may not reflect their true value. Value stocks are considered a conservative investment and are often favored by value investors who are looking for a good deal.

Value stocks are often less volatile than growth stocks, but they may offer lower potential returns. However, if the company's true value is recognized by the market, value stocks can offer significant potential returns.

Dividend Stocks:

Dividend stocks are shares in companies that pay dividends to their shareholders. Dividends are a portion of a company's earnings that are distributed to shareholders on a regular basis. Dividend stocks are considered a conservative investment and are often favored by income investors who are looking for a reliable stream of income.

Dividend stocks are often less volatile than other types of stocks, and they can offer a reliable stream of income even during market downturns. However, they may also offer lower potential returns than other types of stocks.

Conclusion:

When it comes to investing in stocks, there are many different types to consider. Each type of stock has its own unique characteristics, advantages, and risks. Understanding the differences between common stocks

Investing 101: A Beginner's Guide to Building Wealth

CHAPTER 3 - INVESTING IN STOCKS

- ❖ Fundamental Analysis
- ❖ Technical Analysis
- ❖ How to Choose the Right Stocks
- ❖ Risks and Rewards of Investing in Stocks
- ❖ Strategies for Investing in Stocks

Investing in stocks can be a great way to build wealth over time. Whether you're a seasoned investor or just starting out, it's important to have a clear understanding of the different types of stocks, the various approaches to analyzing them, and the potential risks and rewards of investing in them.

In this chapter, we'll explore two primary methods for analyzing stocks: fundamental analysis and technical analysis. Fundamental analysis involves looking at a company's financial statements, industry trends, and other key data to determine whether it is a good investment. Technical analysis, on the other hand, involves analyzing a stock's price movements and other market data to identify trends and patterns that can help predict future performance.

We'll also discuss how to choose the right stocks for your portfolio. This involves considering factors such as your risk tolerance, investment goals, and the current state of the stock market. In addition, we'll cover the potential risks and rewards of investing in stocks, including the potential for high returns and the possibility of significant losses.

Finally, we'll review several strategies for investing in stocks. Whether you're looking to build a long-term portfolio or engage in more active trading, there are a variety of strategies you can use to help achieve your goals. By understanding the different options available to you, you can make informed decisions that will help you succeed in the stock market.

Fundamental Analysis

Investing in stocks can be a lucrative way to grow your wealth over time, but it can also be a risky endeavor. One way to reduce the risks involved is by using fundamental analysis to evaluate stocks and make informed investment decisions.

Fundamental analysis is a method of evaluating a company's financial and economic health to determine its value and potential for growth. This type of analysis looks at a company's financial statements, including its income statement, balance sheet, and cash flow statement, as well as economic and industry data, to determine whether a stock is undervalued or overvalued.

There are several key factors that fundamental analysts consider when evaluating a stock:

Revenue and earnings: The most important factors in fundamental analysis are a company's revenue and earnings. Investors look for companies that have consistent revenue growth, as well as high and growing earnings per share (EPS).

Profitability: Fundamental analysts also consider a company's profitability. This includes metrics such as profit margin, return on equity (ROE), and return on assets (ROA). Companies with high profit margins and strong ROE and ROA are generally seen as good investments.

Debt and leverage: Companies with high levels of debt and leverage are generally seen as riskier investments, as they are more vulnerable to economic downturns and financial crises. Fundamental analysts look at a company's debt-to-equity ratio and interest coverage ratio to evaluate its financial stability.

Valuation: Finally, fundamental analysts consider a company's valuation, or its price-to-earnings (P/E) ratio. A low P/E ratio may indicate that a stock is undervalued, while a high P/E ratio may suggest that it is overvalued.

Using fundamental analysis, investors can evaluate the strengths and weaknesses of a company to determine whether it is a good investment. By analyzing a company's financial statements and economic and industry data, investors can identify undervalued stocks with strong growth potential.

However, it's important to note that fundamental analysis is not foolproof, and there are some limitations to this approach. For example, fundamental analysis may not always accurately predict stock prices, as stock prices are also influenced by a variety of external factors, such as global economic conditions and political events.

Additionally, fundamental analysis can be time-consuming and complex, and requires a deep understanding of financial statements and economic data. As a result, many investors choose to use a combination of fundamental analysis and other investment strategies to make informed investment decisions.

Overall, fundamental analysis is an important tool for investors who are looking to evaluate stocks and make informed investment decisions. By carefully analyzing a company's financial statements and economic data, investors can identify undervalued stocks with strong growth potential and make sound investment choices.

Technical Analysis

Technical analysis is a method of evaluating securities by analyzing statistics generated by market activity, such as past prices and volume. It is one of the two main methods of stock analysis, the other being fundamental analysis. Technical analysts believe that the historical price and volume data of a security can be used to identify patterns and predict future price movements.

The underlying principle of technical analysis is that the market is a self-regulating mechanism that reflects all relevant information, including supply and demand, economic trends, and market psychology. Technical analysts focus on the study of price charts, technical indicators, and other statistical tools to forecast the direction of the market and the future price movement of a security.

Price Charts

Price charts are the most basic and widely used tool in technical analysis. A price chart is a graphical representation of a security's price movement over a period of time. The most common types of charts used in technical analysis are line charts, bar charts, and candlestick charts.

Line charts are the simplest form of price charts. They plot a security's closing prices for each trading session as a single line. Bar charts, on the other hand, show the high, low, and closing prices for each trading session as a vertical bar. Candlestick charts are similar to bar charts, but the body of the candlestick is colored to indicate whether the closing price is higher or lower than the opening price.

Technical Indicators

Technical indicators are mathematical calculations based on the price and/or volume of a security. They are used to confirm price trends and the strength of market trends. There are two types of technical indicators: leading indicators and lagging indicators.

Leading indicators are used to predict future price movements based on current market conditions. Examples of leading indicators include the relative strength index (RSI), stochastic oscillator, and moving averages.

Lagging indicators, on the other hand, are used to confirm trends that have already occurred. They are based on past market data and include indicators such as moving averages, Bollinger Bands, and moving average convergence divergence (MACD).

Other Statistical Tools

In addition to price charts and technical indicators, technical analysts also use other statistical tools to evaluate securities. These include:

Volume: The number of shares traded in a security over a given period of time. High volume is often seen as a confirmation of price trends.

Open interest: The number of outstanding contracts in the futures or options markets. High open interest can indicate a strong trend in the underlying security.

Support and resistance levels: These are levels at which the price of a security tends to stop falling (support) or rising (resistance).

Trend lines: These are lines that connect the high or low points of a security's price movement over a given period of time. They are used to identify trends and predict future price movements.

Criticism of Technical Analysis

Critics of technical analysis argue that it is based on the flawed assumption that the market is a self-regulating mechanism that always reflects all relevant information. They also point out that technical analysis is backward-looking and based on historical price data, which may not accurately predict future market trends.

Despite these criticisms, technical analysis is widely used by traders and investors around the world. It is especially popular in the short-term trading of securities, such as stocks, futures, and options. Technical analysis can be a useful tool for traders and investors to identify trends and market patterns, but it should be used in conjunction with other methods of analysis, such as fundamental analysis, and should not be relied on as the sole basis for investment decisions.

How to Choose the Right Stocks

When it comes to investing in stocks, choosing the right stocks to invest in can be a crucial factor in achieving your financial goals. With thousands of stocks available for investment, it can be overwhelming to determine which ones to buy. However, by following a few key principles, you can make informed decisions and increase your chances of success.

Know Your Goals and Risk Tolerance

Before investing in any stock, it is important to understand your investment goals and risk tolerance. Are you investing for short-term gains or long-term growth? Are you willing to take on more risk in exchange for the potential for higher returns, or do you prefer a more conservative approach?

By understanding your goals and risk tolerance, you can narrow down your choices to stocks that align with your investment strategy.

Research the Company

Once you have a clear understanding of your investment goals and risk tolerance, the next step is to research the companies you are interested in investing in. This includes reviewing the company's financial statements, management team, products and services, competition, and industry trends.

In addition, it is important to assess the company's future growth potential. Are there upcoming products or services that may lead to increased revenue and profits? What is the company's market share within its industry?

Look at the Valuation

After researching the company, it is important to assess its valuation. This involves looking at financial ratios such as the price-to-earnings ratio (P/E ratio) and price-to-sales ratio (P/S ratio) to determine whether the stock is overvalued or undervalued.

For example, a company with a high P/E ratio may indicate that the stock is overpriced relative to its earnings, while a low P/E ratio may indicate that the stock is undervalued. However, it is important to consider other factors such as the company's growth potential and industry trends when assessing valuation.

Consider Dividends

Dividends are payments made by companies to their shareholders, typically out of their earnings. Dividend-paying stocks can provide a source of income for investors, as well as the potential for capital appreciation.

When considering dividend-paying stocks, it is important to assess the company's dividend history and its ability to continue paying dividends in the future. This includes reviewing the company's financial statements and management team, as well as its industry trends and competition.

Evaluate the Market

The stock market can be highly volatile, and it is important to assess market conditions when choosing stocks to invest in. This includes analyzing the overall economic environment, as well as industry trends and specific company news.

It is also important to diversify your investments across different sectors and industries to mitigate risk. This can involve investing in different types of stocks, such as growth and value stocks, as well as stocks in different regions and countries.

Monitor Your Investments

Once you have chosen stocks to invest in, it is important to monitor your investments on an ongoing basis. This includes reviewing financial statements and market conditions, as well as assessing your investment goals and risk tolerance over time.

In addition, it may be necessary to adjust your investment strategy as market conditions and personal circumstances change. This can involve rebalancing your portfolio to maintain a diversified mix of stocks, as well as selling stocks that no longer align with your investment goals.

Investing in stocks can be a challenging but rewarding endeavor. By following these key principles for choosing the right stocks, you can make informed decisions and increase your chances of achieving your financial goals.

Risks and Rewards of Investing in Stocks

Investing in stocks can be an exciting way to grow your wealth, but it also involves risks. The stock market can be unpredictable, and it can be difficult to know which stocks to invest in and when to sell. It's essential to understand both the risks and rewards of investing in stocks before putting your money into the market.

Risks of Investing in Stocks

Market Risk: One of the most significant risks of investing in stocks is market risk. The stock market can be unpredictable, and the value of stocks can fluctuate based on factors like economic conditions, company performance, and global events. A sudden downturn in the market can lead to significant losses for investors.

Volatility Risk: Volatility risk is another factor to consider when investing in stocks. Volatility refers to how much the stock price fluctuates over time. Highly volatile stocks can be riskier than more stable stocks.

Business Risk: Business risk refers to the potential for a company to perform poorly or even fail. A company's stock price is tied to its performance, so if the company struggles, the value of its stock can decrease.

Liquidity Risk: Liquidity risk is the risk of not being able to sell your stocks quickly enough at a fair price. Stocks with low trading volumes or low liquidity can be riskier because they may not be easy to sell quickly.

Inflation Risk: Inflation risk refers to the risk that inflation will erode the purchasing power of your investments. This can be a particular concern for investors who rely on their investments for income in retirement.

Rewards of Investing in Stocks

Capital Appreciation: The primary reason most investors put their money into stocks is the potential for capital appreciation. Stocks can increase in value over time, and if you sell your shares at a higher price than you paid for them, you'll realize a profit.

Dividends: Many companies pay dividends to their shareholders. Dividends are regular payments made to shareholders out of a company's profits. Dividend stocks can provide a reliable source of income for investors.

Diversification: Investing in stocks can help diversify your investment portfolio. Holding a mix of stocks in different industries and sectors can help spread out your risk.

Inflation Hedge: Stocks can be a good hedge against inflation because as prices rise, the value of companies and their earnings also tends to rise.

Strategies for Managing Risks and Rewards

Diversification: One way to manage risks is to diversify your portfolio. By holding a mix of stocks, bonds, and other assets, you can spread out your risk and minimize the impact of any one investment's poor performance.

Research: Before investing in any stock, it's important to do your research. Look at the company's financial statements, management team, and industry trends. By understanding the company and its potential, you can make more informed investment decisions.

Long-Term Investing: Investing in stocks should be a long-term strategy. Over time, the stock market has historically provided strong returns, but short-term fluctuations can be unpredictable. By taking a long-term view, you can ride out market fluctuations and benefit from the market's overall growth.

Asset Allocation: Your asset allocation strategy should be based on your investment goals, risk tolerance, and time horizon. Younger investors with a longer time horizon may be comfortable with a more aggressive allocation of stocks, while older investors nearing retirement may prefer a more conservative allocation.

Risks of Investing in Stocks:

Market Risk: Market risk is the risk that your investment will lose value due to overall market conditions. Even well-diversified portfolios can experience losses in a down market.

Company-Specific Risk: Company-specific risk refers to the risk associated with owning individual stocks. The performance of a company, including its earnings, management, and other factors, can significantly affect the value of the stock.

Inflation Risk: Inflation risk is the risk that the value of your investment will be eroded by inflation. Inflation can reduce the purchasing power of your investment returns, especially if your investments are not earning returns that are higher than the rate of inflation.

Interest Rate Risk: Interest rate risk refers to the risk that changes in interest rates will impact the value of your investment. Generally, stocks perform poorly when interest rates rise, as investors prefer the safety of fixed-income investments.

Rewards of Investing in Stocks:

Long-Term Growth Potential: Over the long term, stocks have historically provided higher returns than other asset classes, such as bonds or cash. By investing in a diversified portfolio of stocks, you can potentially earn a return on your investment that outpaces inflation and helps you achieve your financial goals.

Dividend Income: Many stocks pay dividends, which can provide a reliable income stream for investors. By investing in dividend-paying stocks, you can earn income while also participating in the potential growth of the company.

Diversification: By investing in a diverse portfolio of stocks, you can spread your risk across multiple companies and industries. Diversification can help reduce the impact of company-specific risk and market risk on your portfolio.

Investment Strategies:

Buy and Hold: This strategy involves buying stocks and holding them for the long term, with the belief that their value will increase over time. This strategy requires patience and discipline and is well-suited for investors who have a long-term investment horizon.

Dollar-Cost Averaging: This strategy involves investing a fixed dollar amount in stocks at regular intervals, regardless of market conditions. By investing regularly, you can potentially take advantage of market downturns and benefit from the long-term growth potential of the stock market.

Value Investing: Value investing involves looking for stocks that are undervalued by the market, with the belief that their true value will be recognized over time. This strategy requires research and analysis to identify undervalued stocks and may require patience to see the value realized.

Growth Investing: Growth investing involves looking for stocks that have high growth potential, with the belief that their earnings and stock price will increase rapidly. This strategy requires careful analysis of a company's financials and growth potential and may involve taking on more risk than other strategies.

In conclusion, investing in stocks can be an effective way to grow your wealth over time, but it also involves risks. By understanding both the risks and rewards of investing in stocks and implementing sound investment strategies, you can build a diversified investment portfolio and increase your chances of achieving your financial goals. It is important to remember that investing involves risk and there are no guarantees of success.

Conclusion

Investing in stocks can be an exciting and potentially profitable endeavor, but it's important to understand the risks and rewards involved. By using fundamental and technical analysis, as well as choosing the right stocks and diversifying your portfolio, you can minimize your risks and increase your chances of success.

Remember that investing in stocks should be approached with a long-term perspective and that no investment strategy is foolproof. The key is to do your research, make informed decisions, and monitor your portfolio regularly to ensure it aligns with your investment goals and risk tolerance.

With a solid understanding of the various types of stocks, how to analyze them, and how to build a well-diversified portfolio, you can confidently invest in stocks and work towards achieving your financial goals.

PART 2
REAL ESTATE
INVESTMENT

Investing 101: A Beginner's Guide to Building Wealth

CHAPTER 4 - REAL ESTATE INVESTMENT BASICS

❖ What is Real Estate Investment?
❖ The Pros and Cons of Real Estate Investment
❖ Types of Real Estate Investments
❖ Real Estate Investing vs. Stocks
❖ Real Estate Investing vs. Web3

Real estate can be an excellent investment opportunity for those looking to diversify their portfolio or generate passive income. Investing in real estate can involve purchasing and managing properties for rental income or investing in real estate investment trusts (REITs) that own and operate properties. In this chapter, we will explore the basics of real estate investing, including the different types of real estate investments available, the potential risks and rewards, and strategies for success in the real estate market. Whether you're a seasoned investor or just getting started, understanding the fundamentals of real estate investing can help you make informed investment decisions and achieve your financial goals.

What is Real Estate Investment?

The Short Answer

Real estate investment is a popular way to generate income and build wealth. It involves the purchase, ownership, management, rental, or sale of real estate property for profit. This type of investment can include a variety of property types, such as residential and commercial properties, as well as land and buildings.

Investing in real estate can be an attractive option for many reasons. It can provide a steady stream of passive income, offer significant potential for appreciation, and provide various tax benefits. However, like any investment, real estate investment also involves risks and requires careful consideration and planning.

In this chapter, we will explore what real estate investment is, why people invest in it, and the different types of real estate investment options available.

What is Real Estate Investment?

Real estate investment involves the purchase, ownership, management, rental, or sale of real estate property for profit. There are many different types of real estate investments available, each with their own unique characteristics and potential for profitability.

Some common types of real estate investments include:

Rental properties: Rental properties are real estate properties that are purchased with the intention of renting them out to tenants. The goal is to generate a steady stream of rental income, which can provide a reliable source of passive income. Rental properties can include residential properties, such as apartments, single-family homes, and condos, as well as commercial properties, such as office buildings and retail spaces.

Flipping properties: Flipping properties involves purchasing a property, renovating it, and then selling it for a profit. The goal is to purchase the property at a discounted price, make improvements that increase its value, and then sell it for more than the purchase price and renovation costs. This can be a high-risk, high-reward type of real estate investment, as the potential profits can be significant, but the costs and risks can also be high.

Real estate investment trusts (REITs): REITs are companies that own and operate income-producing real estate properties. Investors can purchase shares of REITs, which provide them with a portion of the income generated by the properties owned by the REIT. REITs can be a more accessible way to invest in real estate, as they offer diversification and liquidity, as well as potentially high returns.

Real estate partnerships: Real estate partnerships involve two or more investors pooling their resources to purchase and manage a real estate property. This type of investment can offer the benefits of real estate ownership, such as potential for appreciation and rental income, while also sharing the costs and responsibilities among the partners.

Why Invest in Real Estate?

Real estate investment can offer a variety of benefits for investors. Some of the key reasons why people choose to invest in real estate include:

Potential for appreciation: Real estate can appreciate in value over time, which can lead to significant profits for investors. This can be especially true in markets with high demand and limited supply.

Steady rental income: Rental properties can provide a reliable stream of passive income, which can be especially appealing for those seeking long-term financial security.

Tax benefits: Real estate investment can offer various tax benefits, such as deductions for mortgage interest, property taxes, and depreciation.

Inflation hedge: Real estate can provide a hedge against inflation, as rental income and property values tend to increase over time in response to inflation.

Portfolio diversification: Real estate investment can offer diversification benefits, as it is not necessarily correlated with other asset classes, such as stocks and bonds.

Types of Real Estate Properties

Real estate properties can be divided into two broad categories: residential and commercial.

Residential properties are properties that are designed for living, such as single-family homes, apartments, townhouses, and condominiums. Residential real estate properties are typically owned by individuals or families, and they are usually intended to be used as primary residences or investment properties.

Commercial properties, on the other hand, are properties that are used for business purposes, such as office buildings, retail spaces, industrial buildings, and warehouses. These types of properties are usually owned by corporations or businesses and are intended to generate income through renting or leasing.

Apart from residential and commercial properties, there are also several other types of real estate properties, such as raw land, farms, and vacation properties. Raw land refers to undeveloped land, while farms refer to land that is used for agriculture or raising livestock. Vacation properties, also known as second homes, are typically located in scenic locations and are intended to be used as a retreat or a place for vacation.

Each type of real estate property has its own unique characteristics, advantages, and challenges. Residential properties are generally easier to purchase and maintain, while commercial properties may offer higher returns but require more expertise to manage. Raw land and farms may be ideal for long-term investment, while vacation properties may provide both a rental income and a personal getaway.

As with any investment, it's important to conduct thorough research and due diligence before investing in real estate. This includes researching the local real estate market, understanding zoning laws and regulations, assessing the condition and value of the property, and evaluating potential rental income or resale value. By doing so, you can make informed investment decisions that align with your financial goals and risk tolerance.

The Pros and Cons of Real Estate Investment

Real estate investment has long been a popular choice for individuals looking to diversify their investment portfolio and generate passive income. While there are many benefits to investing in real estate, there are also drawbacks and potential pitfalls to consider. In this chapter, we'll explore the pros and cons of real estate investment to help you make an informed decision about whether this type of investment is right for you.

Pros of Real Estate Investment

Potential for Passive Income

One of the biggest advantages of real estate investment is the potential for passive income. When you invest in rental properties, you can generate ongoing rental income each month. This can be a great way to build wealth over time and create a reliable source of income.

Appreciation in Property Value

Real estate properties typically appreciate in value over time, meaning that the value of your investment can increase as time goes on. This can lead to significant gains in your investment portfolio, and may be especially true in certain markets that experience high levels of demand.

Tax Benefits

Real estate investment can come with a range of tax benefits that can help to offset the costs of owning and maintaining a property. For example, you can deduct expenses such as property taxes, mortgage interest, and repairs and maintenance from your income taxes. Additionally, if you sell a property that you've owned for more than a year, you may be eligible for a lower tax rate on any capital gains.

Inflation Hedge

Real estate investment can also serve as a hedge against inflation. Inflation can erode the value of cash and other assets over time, but real estate tends to hold its value and can even appreciate in value during inflationary periods.

Cons of Real Estate Investment

High Upfront Costs

Real estate investment can require a significant amount of upfront capital, which can make it difficult for some investors to get started. Additionally, the costs of owning and maintaining a property can add up quickly, which can be a barrier for some investors.

Property Management and Maintenance

Owning and managing a rental property can be a time-consuming and complex process. You'll need to find tenants, handle maintenance and repairs, and deal with a range of legal and financial issues. This can be a major source of stress and can require a significant amount of time and effort.

Market Risks

The real estate market can be unpredictable, and property values can fluctuate based on a range of factors such as economic conditions, local supply and demand, and changing interest rates. This can make real estate investment more risky than other types of investments that are more stable and predictable.

Illiquidity

Real estate is generally a less liquid asset than other types of investments such as stocks or bonds. This means that it can be more difficult to sell a property quickly and convert your investment into cash. This lack of liquidity can make real estate investment less suitable for investors who may need to access their funds quickly.

Legal and Regulatory Risks

Real estate investment also comes with a range of legal and regulatory risks. You'll need to comply with a range of local, state, and federal regulations when owning and managing a property, and failure to do so can result in fines and legal liabilities.

Strategies for Mitigating Risks

While there are risks associated with real estate investment, there are also strategies that you can use to mitigate those risks and improve your chances of success. Some strategies to consider include:

Conduct thorough research before investing. This includes researching the local real estate market, analyzing potential properties, and understanding the financial and legal implications of owning and managing a property.

Develop a solid business plan. This should include a detailed financial plan, marketing and tenant acquisition strategies, and plans for property management and maintenance.

Diversifying your real estate portfolio is another important strategy to minimize risk and maximize returns. This means investing in different types of properties across different geographic locations. For example, you may consider investing in both residential and commercial properties, or in properties in different states or even different countries.

Diversification can also mean investing in different investment vehicles, such as real estate investment trusts (REITs), which are companies that own and manage income-generating real estate properties. REITs can offer a more liquid and less hands-on way to invest in real estate, with the potential for consistent dividend payments and long-term capital appreciation.

It's also important to consider diversification within a single property investment. This can be achieved by having multiple tenants, each with their own lease agreement and rental terms. This helps to spread out the risk of vacancies and late payments, and can also provide a steady stream of income.

Consider the costs and fees associated with real estate investment

Investing in real estate can come with various costs and fees that should be carefully considered. These can include the upfront costs of purchasing a property, such as down payments, closing costs, and inspection fees, as well as ongoing expenses such as property taxes, insurance, maintenance, and repairs.

It's important to factor in these costs when evaluating the potential returns on a real estate investment. It's also important to consider the costs of hiring a property management company or real estate agent, as well as the potential costs of vacancies and non-paying tenants.

Another cost to consider is the opportunity cost of tying up your capital in a real estate investment. Real estate investments can be illiquid and may take time to sell, which can limit your ability to quickly access your funds if needed.

Understand the legal and regulatory requirements of real estate investment

Real estate investment is subject to a range of legal and regulatory requirements, including zoning laws, building codes, and tenant rights laws. It's important to be aware of these requirements and ensure compliance to avoid legal and financial penalties.

It's also important to have a solid understanding of real estate contracts and legal documents, such as purchase agreements, lease agreements, and property management contracts. Consulting with a real estate attorney can be helpful to ensure that all legal requirements are met and to protect your interests as a real estate investor.

Conclusion

Real estate investment can be a lucrative way to build long-term wealth, but it requires careful consideration, research, and planning. By understanding the pros and cons of real estate investment, developing a solid investment strategy, and carefully evaluating potential investment opportunities, investors can minimize risk and maximize returns in the real estate market. It's important to remember that real estate investment is a long-term commitment that requires ongoing management and attention, and that there are costs and risks associated with any investment.

Types of Real Estate Investments

Real estate investments come in different shapes and sizes, and each one has its own set of pros and cons. Here are some of the most common types of real estate investments:

Rental Properties

Rental properties are a popular choice for real estate investors. This type of investment involves purchasing a property with the intention of renting it out to tenants. Rental properties can include single-family homes, apartments, and commercial properties. The income generated from renting out the property can provide a steady stream of passive income for the investor.

One of the advantages of rental properties is that they can provide a hedge against inflation, as rents tend to rise with inflation. However, rental properties can also be time-consuming to manage, requiring ongoing maintenance and dealing with tenant issues.

Real Estate Investment Trusts (REITs)

Real Estate Investment Trusts (REITs) are companies that own and manage income-producing real estate properties. REITs are a popular choice for investors who want exposure to the real estate market but don't want to deal with the hassle of owning and managing properties themselves.

REITs are required by law to distribute at least 90% of their taxable income to shareholders, making them an attractive option for investors seeking regular income. However, the performance of a REIT is dependent on the performance of the real estate market, which can be volatile.

Real Estate Mutual Funds

Real estate mutual funds are similar to REITs in that they provide investors with exposure to the real estate market without requiring them to manage properties themselves. Real estate mutual funds invest in a portfolio of publicly traded real estate companies, such as REITs and homebuilders.

One of the advantages of real estate mutual funds is that they offer diversification, as they invest in a broad range of real estate companies. However, like REITs, the performance of real estate mutual funds is tied to the performance of the real estate market.

Flipping Properties

Flipping properties involves buying a property, making renovations or improvements, and then selling it for a profit. This type of investment can be risky, as it requires a lot of upfront capital and expertise in real estate and construction.

The potential upside of flipping properties is that it can generate substantial profits in a short amount of time. However, it can also be time-consuming and stressful, as investors must find the right property to flip and manage the renovation process.

Real Estate Crowdfunding

Real estate crowdfunding is a relatively new type of real estate investment that involves pooling money from multiple investors to fund a real estate project. Crowdfunding platforms connect investors with real estate developers and operators, allowing them to invest in projects that were previously only available to institutional investors.

One of the advantages of real estate crowdfunding is that it allows investors to invest in real estate with relatively small amounts of capital. However, it can be risky, as investors are investing in a project rather than a tangible asset like a property.

In conclusion, there are many different types of real estate investments available to investors, each with its own set of advantages and disadvantages. When deciding which type of real estate investment to pursue, it's important to consider your goals, risk tolerance, and expertise in real estate.

Real Estate Investing vs. Stocks

Real estate investing and stock investing are two popular options for building wealth. Both investment strategies have their own unique benefits and drawbacks, making it important for investors to weigh their options carefully before choosing which route to take.

In this chapter, we will explore the similarities and differences between real estate investing and stock investing, as well as the pros and cons of each.

Real Estate Investing

Real estate investing involves purchasing a property with the intention of earning a return on investment. This can be achieved through various methods, such as rental income, property appreciation, or flipping.

One of the primary benefits of real estate investing is the potential for stable, long-term income. Rental properties can provide a steady stream of income in the form of monthly rent payments, which can be used to pay off mortgage loans, cover property expenses, and generate profits. Real estate also has the potential for appreciation over time, allowing investors to profit from increases in property values.

However, real estate investing also comes with some unique challenges and risks. For example, property management can be time-consuming and costly, especially if investors choose to manage the property themselves. Additionally, real estate markets can be unpredictable, with factors such as economic conditions and local zoning laws affecting property values and demand.

Stock Investing

Stock investing involves purchasing shares of publicly traded companies with the goal of earning a return on investment. This can be achieved through capital gains, which occur when the value of a stock increases, or through dividends, which are regular payments made to shareholders from a company's profits.

One of the primary benefits of stock investing is the potential for high returns. Historically, stocks have outperformed other types of investments over the long-term, with average annual returns of around 10%. Additionally, stock investing is generally more liquid than real estate investing, with shares being easily bought and sold on public exchanges.

However, stock investing also comes with its own unique risks and challenges. The stock market can be volatile, with sudden fluctuations in share prices due to factors such as economic conditions, company performance, and global events. This can lead to significant losses for investors who are not well-versed in market trends and investing strategies.

Real Estate vs. Stock Investing: Pros and Cons

When considering whether to invest in real estate or stocks, it's important to weigh the pros and cons of each strategy.

Real Estate Investing Pros:

Potential for long-term, stable income from rental properties
Potential for property appreciation and profits from selling properties
Diversification from other types of investments, such as stocks and bonds

Real Estate Investing Cons:

Property management can be time-consuming and costly
Real estate markets can be unpredictable, with factors such as local zoning laws affecting property values and demand
Requires a significant amount of capital to purchase properties

Stock Investing Pros:

Potential for high returns over the long-term

More liquid than real estate, with shares being easily bought and sold

Access to a wide range of companies and industries

Stock Investing Cons:

The stock market can be volatile, with sudden fluctuations in share prices

High levels of market speculation and uncertainty

Can be challenging to understand and analyze market trends and individual companies

Which is the Better Investment?

The decision of whether to invest in real estate or stocks ultimately depends on a variety of factors, including an individual's financial goals, risk tolerance, and investment experience.

Some investors may prefer the stability and predictability of real estate investing, while others may be drawn to the potentially higher returns of stock investing. It's also possible to diversify one's portfolio by investing in both real estate and stocks, which can help to mitigate the risks of each investment strategy.

Ultimately, the key to successful investing is to conduct thorough research, develop a sound investment plan, and remain disciplined in executing that plan. Regardless of whether an individual chooses to invest in real estate, stocks, or a combination of both, the fundamental principles of investing still apply.

Investing in real estate and stocks both offer unique advantages and disadvantages. Real estate investing provides the opportunity for long-term passive income through rental properties, and the potential for appreciation in property values over time. It can also offer a tangible asset that can be used as collateral for financing or sold for a profit. However, real estate investments require a significant amount of capital upfront and may involve ongoing expenses for maintenance, property management, and tenant acquisition.

Investing in stocks, on the other hand, provides the potential for high returns through stock price appreciation, as well as dividend income from certain stocks. It also offers a higher degree of liquidity, as stocks can be bought and sold easily on exchanges. However, stock prices can be volatile and subject to market fluctuations, and there is no guarantee of a return on investment.

When deciding between real estate and stocks, it's important to consider personal preferences, investment goals, and risk tolerance. Real estate investments may be more suitable for those who are comfortable with a longer-term investment horizon and have the financial resources to cover the initial expenses. Stocks may be more appropriate for those seeking higher potential returns and are comfortable with the inherent risks of the stock market.

Ultimately, a well-diversified investment portfolio should include a mix of both real estate and stocks, as well as other asset classes such as bonds and mutual funds. By diversifying across a range of investments, investors can help to mitigate risk and potentially maximize returns over the long term.

In conclusion, the decision between investing in real estate or stocks is not a one-size-fits-all approach. Each investment type offers its own unique benefits and drawbacks, and the decision ultimately depends on an individual's personal financial goals and risk tolerance. Regardless of the choice, it's important to conduct thorough research, develop a solid investment plan, and remain disciplined in executing that plan in order to achieve long-term success.

Real Estate Investing vs. Web3

Real estate investing has been a popular investment option for many years, but the emergence of Web3 and blockchain technology has brought a new investment opportunity to the forefront. Web3, also known as the decentralized web, is a new internet infrastructure that uses blockchain technology to create a more open, transparent, and secure internet.

While real estate investing and Web3 investing are different in many ways, there are also some similarities between the two. In this chapter, we will explore the key differences and similarities between real estate investing and Web3 investing.

Real Estate Investing

Real estate investing involves purchasing, owning, and managing real estate properties in order to generate income and/or capital appreciation. Real estate investments can take many forms, including rental properties, commercial properties, and land. Real estate investors typically make money through rental income, appreciation in property values, and/or the sale of the property.

Real estate investing has traditionally been a popular investment option due to its potential for steady cash flow, long-term capital appreciation, and the ability to use leverage to amplify returns. Real estate investing also offers some tax benefits, including the ability to deduct mortgage interest and depreciation.

However, real estate investing also comes with some risks. Real estate prices can be volatile and can be affected by changes in interest rates, economic conditions, and local real estate market conditions. Real estate investments also require a significant amount of capital, as well as time and effort to manage properties, find tenants, and maintain the property.

Web3 Investing

Web3 investing involves investing in decentralized applications (dApps) and cryptocurrencies built on blockchain technology. This can include investments in cryptocurrencies such as Bitcoin, Ethereum, and other altcoins, as well as investments in decentralized finance (DeFi) applications, non-fungible tokens (NFTs), and other decentralized applications.

Web3 investing is a relatively new investment option, but it has grown rapidly in popularity due to its potential for high returns and the innovative nature of the technology. Web3 investing offers the potential for high returns due to the high volatility of cryptocurrencies and the potential for rapid growth in the value of decentralized applications.

However, Web3 investing also comes with significant risks. The price of cryptocurrencies can be highly volatile and can be affected by a wide range of factors, including regulatory changes, market sentiment, and technological developments. Investing in Web3 also requires a significant amount of knowledge and understanding of the technology and the market, as well as the ability to navigate the complex regulatory environment.

Real Estate Investing vs. Web3

While real estate investing and Web3 investing are different in many ways, there are also some similarities between the two. Both forms of investing require a significant amount of capital, time, and effort to be successful. They also both offer the potential for high returns, but also come with significant risks.

One key difference between real estate investing and Web3 investing is the level of liquidity. Real estate investments are generally less liquid than Web3 investments, as they typically require a significant amount of time and effort to sell a property. Web3 investments, on the other hand, can be bought and sold quickly on cryptocurrency exchanges.

Another key difference is the level of regulation. Real estate investing is subject to a wide range of regulations, including zoning laws, building codes, and landlord-tenant laws. Web3 investing, on the other hand, is still largely unregulated, which can create significant risks for investors.

Ultimately, the decision to invest in real estate or Web3 will depend on an individual's financial goals, risk tolerance, and investment experience. Both forms of investing offer potential benefits, but also come with significant risks. It is important to conduct thorough research and due diligence before making any investment decisions.

CHAPTER 5 - TYPES OF REAL ESTATE INVESTMENTS

- ❖ Residential Real Estate
- ❖ Commercial Real Estate
- ❖ Industrial Real Estate
- ❖ Retail Real Estate
- ❖ Mixed-Use Real Estate

Real estate investing offers a variety of options for investors to explore, each with its own set of unique advantages and disadvantages. From residential properties to commercial and industrial buildings, retail spaces to mixed-use developments, there are many different types of real estate investments available to suit different investment goals and risk tolerances.

In this chapter, we will explore the different types of real estate investments available, including their key characteristics, potential returns, and associated risks. We'll take a closer look at residential real estate, commercial real estate, industrial real estate, retail real estate, and mixed-use real estate, providing insights into the investment potential of each type of property. Whether you're looking to invest in rental properties or purchase commercial real estate, this chapter will provide a comprehensive overview of the different types of real estate investments to consider.

Residential Real Estate

Residential real estate refers to properties that are designed for living, such as single-family homes, townhouses, condominiums, and apartment buildings. Residential real estate can be a popular investment for individuals who are interested in generating rental income or who are looking for a long-term investment with the potential for appreciation.

One of the key benefits of investing in residential real estate is the relatively stable demand for rental housing. Many people choose to rent rather than buy a home, which means that rental properties can provide a steady source of income for landlords.

Residential real estate can also be a good investment for those who are interested in long-term appreciation. Over time, the value of residential properties tends to increase, which can result in significant returns for investors who hold onto their properties for several years or even decades.

However, investing in residential real estate is not without risks. For example, vacancies can be a significant challenge for landlords, as they can result in lost rental income and increased maintenance costs. Additionally, managing a rental property can be time-consuming and require a significant amount of effort and expertise.

When investing in residential real estate, it's important to carefully evaluate potential properties and to understand the local rental market. Factors to consider may include the location of the property, the age and condition of the building, the rental history of the property, and the local supply and demand for rental housing.

Overall, investing in residential real estate can be a sound investment strategy for those who are willing to put in the time and effort required to manage a rental property. By carefully selecting properties and developing a sound business plan, investors can potentially generate steady rental income and long-term appreciation.

Commercial Real Estate

Commercial real estate refers to properties that are used for business purposes. These properties can include office buildings, retail stores, warehouses, and other commercial properties. Investing in commercial real estate can be an attractive option for investors seeking long-term returns and diversification of their investment portfolio.

There are several factors that make commercial real estate a compelling investment opportunity. One of the main advantages of investing in commercial real estate is the potential for high rental income. Commercial tenants typically sign longer leases than residential tenants, which means that commercial properties can generate a more stable and predictable stream of rental income. Additionally, commercial tenants are often responsible for paying a portion of the property's operating expenses, such as property taxes and maintenance costs, which can reduce the financial burden on the property owner.

Another advantage of investing in commercial real estate is the potential for capital appreciation. Over time, commercial properties can appreciate in value, providing the potential for significant long-term gains. Commercial properties are often valued based on the property's income, so an increase in rental income can lead to an increase in the property's value.

However, investing in commercial real estate also involves certain risks. One of the main risks is the potential for a lack of tenant demand, which can lead to higher vacancy rates and lower rental income. Economic downturns and changes in the local real estate market can also impact demand for commercial properties, which can negatively affect the property's value and rental income.

Investing in commercial real estate also requires a significant amount of capital and expertise. Commercial properties can be expensive to purchase and require ongoing maintenance and management. Additionally, investing in commercial real estate often involves working with lenders, brokers, and other professionals, which can add to the complexity of the investment.

Despite these risks, commercial real estate can be a profitable investment option for those willing to do their research and invest with a long-term mindset. When considering investing in commercial real estate, it's important to conduct thorough research on the local market, property location, and tenant demand. Additionally, it's important to have a solid understanding of the financial and legal aspects of commercial real estate investing, including financing options, tax implications, and property management strategies.

Investing in commercial real estate can provide a way to diversify an investment portfolio, generate stable income, and potentially achieve long-term gains through capital appreciation. However, it's important to approach commercial real estate investing with caution and to seek the advice of professionals when making investment decisions.

Industrial Real Estate

Industrial real estate is a type of commercial real estate that is specifically designed and used for industrial purposes. Industrial properties are typically large buildings or warehouses that are used for manufacturing, distribution, storage, or research and development. This type of real estate investment can offer attractive returns, but it also comes with its own unique set of risks and challenges.

Industrial properties can be found in a variety of locations, from urban centers to rural areas. They are often situated near transportation hubs, such as ports, highways, or rail lines, to facilitate the transportation of goods and materials. The size of industrial properties can vary widely, from small facilities of a few thousand square feet to large complexes with millions of square feet.

One of the key advantages of investing in industrial real estate is the potential for high rental yields. Industrial tenants typically sign long-term leases, and rental rates are generally higher than for other types of commercial real estate, such as office or retail properties. This can provide a stable source of rental income for investors, even in a down market.

Another advantage of investing in industrial real estate is the potential for capital appreciation. Industrial properties can be improved through upgrades or renovations, which can increase their value over time. Additionally, industrial properties are often located in areas that are experiencing economic growth, which can drive up demand for industrial space and increase property values.

However, there are also several risks associated with investing in industrial real estate. One of the main risks is the potential for vacancy or low occupancy rates. If a tenant vacates an industrial property, it can be difficult to find a replacement tenant quickly, especially if the property is located in a less desirable area. Additionally, industrial properties require specialized knowledge and expertise to manage, and investors may need to hire experienced property managers to handle day-to-day operations.

Investing in industrial real estate also requires a significant amount of capital. Industrial properties can be expensive to purchase and maintain, and investors may need to take on significant debt in order to acquire these properties. Additionally, industrial properties require ongoing maintenance and repairs, which can be costly.

Despite these risks, industrial real estate can be a valuable addition to a diversified investment portfolio. By conducting thorough research, developing a solid investment plan, and working with experienced professionals, investors can successfully navigate the complexities of industrial real estate investing and potentially earn attractive returns over the long term.

Retail Real Estate

Retail real estate refers to commercial properties that are used for retail activities such as shopping, dining, and entertainment. These properties are typically located in areas with high foot traffic and easy access to transportation.

Examples of retail real estate include shopping malls, strip malls, outlet centers, and standalone stores. Retail real estate can be an attractive investment for investors due to the potential for high rental income and capital appreciation.

One of the key benefits of investing in retail real estate is the steady cash flow that comes from rental income. Retail tenants typically sign long-term leases, ranging from five to twenty years, providing a stable and predictable source of rental income for the property owner.

In addition to rental income, retail real estate can also appreciate in value over time, allowing investors to realize capital gains when they sell the property. The value of retail real estate is often determined by the quality of the location, the tenant mix, and the overall condition of the property.

However, investing in retail real estate also comes with its own set of risks. One of the biggest risks is the potential for high vacancy rates, especially in times of economic downturns or shifts in consumer behavior. Retail tenants can also be more prone to failure than other types of commercial tenants, such as office or industrial tenants.

Retail real estate investors need to be aware of trends and changes in consumer behavior, such as the rise of e-commerce, which has led to a decline in brick-and-mortar retail. Investors need to be able to adapt to these changes by finding new tenants or repurposing the property for other uses.

Another risk associated with retail real estate is the need for ongoing maintenance and improvements. Retail properties require regular maintenance, upgrades, and renovations to remain competitive and attract tenants. Investors need to be prepared to make these investments to keep the property in good condition and maintain rental income.

Overall, retail real estate can be a lucrative investment for those willing to take on the risks and challenges that come with owning and managing these types of properties. By conducting thorough research, choosing high-quality properties with strong tenant mixes, and staying on top of trends in the retail industry, investors can maximize their returns and build a successful real estate portfolio.

Mixed-Use Real Estate

Mixed-use real estate refers to properties that combine two or more different uses, such as residential, commercial, and industrial.

These types of properties are becoming increasingly popular as they offer a range of benefits for developers, investors, and tenants.

Mixed-use developments can include a combination of residential apartments, retail space, restaurants, offices, and even recreational areas such as parks and playgrounds. These types of properties can provide a sense of community and a convenient lifestyle for residents, as well as a range of amenities that are attractive to potential tenants.

One of the main advantages of mixed-use developments is their ability to generate higher rental yields compared to single-use properties. With multiple revenue streams from different uses, these properties can provide a more stable income stream for investors.

In addition, mixed-use properties can help to revitalize urban areas, creating more vibrant and attractive communities. These types of developments can attract new businesses and residents, leading to economic growth and job creation.

However, there are also some challenges associated with mixed-use developments. These properties require careful planning and zoning to ensure that the different uses are compatible and do not create conflicts. There may also be higher construction and development costs, as well as the challenge of managing multiple uses and tenants.

Overall, mixed-use real estate can be a lucrative and rewarding investment opportunity for those who are willing to take on the challenges of this complex and diverse type of property. It's important to work with experienced professionals, conduct thorough research and due diligence, and develop a sound investment strategy to ensure long-term success in this sector.

Conclusion

In conclusion, real estate investment offers many different options and types, each with its own benefits and drawbacks. It's essential to choose a type of real estate investment that aligns with your investment goals, financial situation, and risk tolerance. Whether it's residential real estate, commercial real estate, industrial real estate, retail real estate, or mixed-use real estate, thorough research and careful planning are key to success. By investing wisely and remaining patient, you can build a diversified real estate investment portfolio that can help you achieve your long-term financial goals.

CHAPTER 6 - INVESTING IN REAL ESTATE

* ❖ How to Invest in Real Estate
* ❖ Financing Real Estate Investments
* ❖ Tax Benefits of Real Estate Investments
* ❖ Risks and Rewards of Real Estate Investments
* ❖ Strategies for Investing in Real Estate

Investing in real estate can be a profitable way to build wealth, generate passive income, and diversify your investment portfolio. However, it's important to understand the unique aspects of real estate investing and the risks and rewards involved. In this chapter, we'll cover how to invest in real estate, including financing options and tax benefits. We'll also discuss the risks and rewards of real estate investments, and provide strategies for investing in real estate that can help you achieve your financial goals.

How to Invest in Real Estate

Investing in real estate can be a complex and multifaceted process, but with the right knowledge and strategies, it can also be a rewarding and profitable venture. Here are some key steps to consider when investing in real estate:

Determine your goals and investment strategy: Before you start investing in real estate, it's important to define your financial goals and investment strategy. This includes deciding on the type of property you want to invest in, the location, the amount you're willing to spend, and the return on investment you're looking to achieve. Additionally, you'll want to consider your risk tolerance and time horizon for the investment.

Conduct thorough market research: Once you have a clear investment strategy in mind, it's important to research the local real estate market to gain a deeper understanding of the supply and demand for properties in the area. You can use tools like online real estate databases, property management companies, and real estate agents to research property prices, rental rates, vacancy rates, and other market data.

Identify potential properties: After conducting market research, you'll want to identify potential investment properties that meet your criteria. This can involve attending open houses, working with real estate agents, or even contacting property owners directly. When evaluating potential properties, consider factors like location, condition, age, size, and potential for future appreciation.

Conduct due diligence: Once you've identified a potential investment property, it's important to conduct due diligence to ensure that the property meets your investment criteria and is free of any legal or financial issues. This can involve hiring a professional inspector to examine the property, reviewing financial records and tax information, and conducting a title search to verify ownership.

Secure financing: After you've identified a potential investment property and conducted due diligence, the next step is to secure financing. This can involve obtaining a mortgage from a bank or financial institution, or using alternative financing options like private lending or real estate crowdfunding. It's important to consider the interest rates, fees, and other costs associated with financing, as well as the potential risks of borrowing.

Close the deal: Once you've secured financing, you'll need to finalize the purchase of the property by signing a purchase agreement and closing the deal. This typically involves working with a real estate attorney and a title company to transfer ownership of the property and ensure that all legal and financial requirements are met.

Manage and maintain the property: After you've acquired an investment property, it's important to manage and maintain the property to ensure that it remains a profitable investment. This can involve tasks like finding and screening tenants, collecting rent, maintaining the property, and handling any legal or financial issues that arise.

By following these steps and conducting thorough research and due diligence, you can successfully invest in real estate and achieve your financial goals. It's important to remain patient and disciplined, and to continuously evaluate your investment strategy to ensure that it aligns with your changing goals and risk tolerance.

Financing Real Estate Investments

Financing real estate investments is a crucial aspect of investing in real estate, as it can help investors access the capital necessary to acquire, renovate, or develop properties. In this chapter, we will explore the various methods of financing real estate investments and their pros and cons.

Cash

One of the most straightforward methods of financing a real estate investment is to pay for the property in cash. This means the investor is using their own money to fund the purchase, without taking on any debt. While this approach can offer several benefits, such as avoiding interest payments and enabling quick transactions, it may not be feasible for everyone.

For instance, real estate properties can be quite expensive, and most investors may not have the cash on hand to purchase a property outright. Additionally, tying up a significant portion of one's cash reserves in a single investment may not be the most prudent financial decision.

Mortgages

Mortgages are one of the most common methods of financing real estate investments, and they work by providing the investor with a loan to purchase a property. The loan is secured by the property itself, and the investor must make regular payments to repay the loan with interest over a set period.

One of the benefits of using a mortgage to finance a real estate investment is that it allows investors to acquire properties that they may not be able to purchase outright. Mortgages also offer relatively low-interest rates compared to other types of loans, making them an attractive financing option.

However, mortgages also come with certain risks and drawbacks. If the investor is unable to make the required payments, they risk losing the property to foreclosure. Mortgages also require a significant amount of documentation and can be time-consuming to obtain.

Hard Money Loans

Hard money loans are a type of short-term loan that is often used to finance real estate investments. These loans are typically offered by private lenders and are secured by the property itself. Hard money loans can be beneficial for investors who need to acquire or renovate a property quickly or who do not qualify for traditional mortgages.

One of the key benefits of hard money loans is their quick approval process. In some cases, investors can receive funding within a few days of applying for the loan. Additionally, hard money loans are often less concerned with an investor's creditworthiness than traditional mortgages, which can be helpful for those with lower credit scores.

However, hard money loans typically come with higher interest rates and fees than traditional mortgages. Additionally, they often have shorter repayment terms, which can make them more challenging to manage for some investors.

Private Money Loans

Private money loans are another financing option for real estate investors. These loans are similar to hard money loans in that they are offered by private lenders and are typically secured by the property itself. However, private money loans can be more flexible than hard money loans, and the terms of the loan can be negotiated between the investor and the lender.

Private money loans can be beneficial for investors who need more flexibility than traditional mortgages offer. For instance, the loan terms can be customized to fit the specific needs of the investor or property. Additionally, private money loans often have faster approval times than traditional mortgages.

However, private money loans can come with higher interest rates and fees than traditional mortgages, and the lender may require a significant down payment or collateral to secure the loan.

Crowdfunding

Crowdfunding has become an increasingly popular method of financing real estate investments in recent years. Crowdfunding platforms allow investors to pool their funds with other investors to finance the purchase or development of a property.

One of the benefits of crowdfunding is that it allows investors to access real estate opportunities that they may not have been able to access on their own. Crowdfunding can also offer relatively low minimum investment requirements, making it a more accessible option for some investors.

However, crowdfunding also comes with its own set of risks. Investors may have limited control over the specific properties in which their funds are invested, and may have to rely on the expertise and judgement of the crowdfunding platform and its operators. Additionally, some crowdfunding platforms may have high fees or other hidden costs that can eat into an investor's returns.

Real Estate Investment Trusts (REITs)

Real estate investment trusts, or REITs, are companies that own or finance income-producing real estate properties. They offer a way for individual investors to invest in real estate without actually owning the physical properties themselves. Instead, investors can purchase shares of the REIT, which represents an ownership stake in the underlying properties.

One of the benefits of REITs is that they offer relatively high levels of liquidity, since shares can be bought and sold on public stock exchanges. REITs can also offer relatively high dividend yields, since they are required to distribute at least 90% of their taxable income to shareholders in the form of dividends.

However, REITs also come with their own set of risks. Like with crowdfunding, investors may have limited control over the specific properties in which their funds are invested. Additionally, some REITs may be more heavily leveraged than others, which can increase their exposure to market downturns or other economic risks.

Private Equity Funds

Private equity funds are investment vehicles that pool capital from individual investors and use it to invest in a range of assets, including real estate properties. These funds are typically managed by professional investment managers, who use their expertise to identify and invest in promising real estate opportunities.

One of the benefits of private equity funds is that they can offer high potential returns, since they have more flexibility to invest in a wider range of properties and to use more complex investment strategies. Private equity funds can also offer more control to investors, since they typically require larger minimum investments and offer more detailed information about the specific properties in which they are investing.

However, private equity funds can also come with their own set of risks. They may require larger minimum investments than other real estate investment options, which can make them less accessible to some investors. Additionally, the management fees and other costs associated with private equity funds can be relatively high, which can eat into an investor's potential returns.

Conclusion:

Real estate investments can offer a range of benefits to individual investors, including potential returns, diversification, and tax benefits.

However, each type of real estate investment comes with its own set of risks and rewards, and investors should carefully evaluate their options before deciding where to invest their money.

By conducting thorough research, developing a sound investment plan, and remaining patient and disciplined in their approach, investors can build a diversified real estate portfolio that meets their financial goals and risk tolerance.

Tax Benefits of Real Estate Investments

Real estate investments can be an excellent way to grow your wealth over time, and one of the biggest advantages of investing in real estate is the numerous tax benefits that it offers. In this chapter, we will explore the various tax benefits of real estate investments, including deductions, exemptions, and credits.

Depreciation Deduction

One of the most significant tax benefits of real estate investing is the depreciation deduction. This is a tax deduction that allows real estate investors to deduct a portion of the cost of a property from their taxable income over the property's useful life.

For example, suppose an investor purchases a rental property for $500,000. In that case, they can deduct a portion of the property's cost, typically 1/27.5 of the property's value, from their taxable income each year for the next 27.5 years. This can significantly reduce the investor's tax liability, especially in the early years of ownership when the property is generating less income.

Mortgage Interest Deduction

Another significant tax benefit of real estate investing is the mortgage interest deduction. This allows real estate investors to deduct the interest paid on their mortgage from their taxable income. The deduction is available for mortgages up to $750,000, and it applies to both primary residences and investment properties.

For example, suppose an investor takes out a mortgage of $500,000 to purchase a rental property. In that case, they can deduct the interest paid on the mortgage from their taxable income. This deduction can significantly reduce the investor's tax liability and make real estate investing even more attractive.

Property Taxes Deduction

Real estate investors can also deduct the property taxes they pay on their investment properties from their taxable income. This deduction can be especially significant for investors with multiple properties or properties in areas with high property tax rates.

For example, suppose an investor owns three rental properties and pays a total of $10,000 in property taxes each year. In that case, they can deduct that $10,000 from their taxable income, reducing their tax liability.

1031 Exchange

A 1031 exchange is a tax-deferred exchange that allows real estate investors to sell a property and reinvest the proceeds in a similar property without paying capital gains taxes. To qualify for a 1031 exchange, the investor must reinvest the proceeds in a like-kind property within 180 days.

For example, suppose an investor sells a rental property for $1 million, generating a $500,000 capital gain. In that case, they can reinvest that $1 million in a like-kind property and defer paying taxes on the $500,000 capital gain.

Capital Gains Tax

Capital gains tax is a tax on the profit made from the sale of an investment property. The tax rate varies depending on the length of time the property was held and the investor's tax bracket. However, if the property is held for more than a year, the tax rate is typically lower than the rate for short-term capital gains.

For example, suppose an investor sells a rental property for $1 million, generating a $500,000 capital gain. If the property was held for more than a year, the investor may qualify for a lower tax rate on the capital gain.

Passive Activity Losses

Real estate investors can also deduct passive activity losses from their taxable income. Passive activity losses occur when the expenses of a rental property exceed the income generated by that property.

For example, suppose an investor owns a rental property that generates $10,000 in income each year but incurs $15,000 in expenses. In that case, they can deduct the $5,000 loss from their taxable income.

Tax Credits

Tax credits are another way that real estate investors can reduce their tax liability. A tax credit is a dollar-for-dollar reduction in the amount of tax owed. Unlike deductions, which reduce the amount of taxable income, tax credits directly reduce the amount of tax owed.

There are several tax credits that real estate investors can take advantage of, including:

Low-Income Housing Tax Credit (LIHTC)

The LIHTC is a federal tax credit that is designed to incentivize real estate investors to develop affordable housing for low-income households. The credit is equal to a percentage of the cost of developing the affordable housing, and can be claimed over a period of 10 years.

To qualify for the LIHTC, investors must develop affordable housing units that meet certain criteria, such as rent restrictions and income limits for tenants. The LIHTC can be a valuable tool for investors who are looking to make a positive impact in their communities while also taking advantage of tax benefits.

Historic Rehabilitation Tax Credit

The Historic Rehabilitation Tax Credit is a federal tax credit that is designed to encourage the rehabilitation and preservation of historic buildings. The credit is equal to a percentage of the cost of rehabilitating a historic building, and can be claimed over a period of five years.

To qualify for the Historic Rehabilitation Tax Credit, the building must be listed on the National Register of Historic Places or be located in a registered historic district. Investors must also meet certain requirements related to the amount of money invested in the rehabilitation and the amount of work done on the building.

Energy Tax Credits

Energy tax credits are designed to incentivize real estate investors to make energy-efficient improvements to their properties. There are several different energy tax credits that investors can take advantage of, including:

Residential Energy Efficiency Property Credit: This credit is available to homeowners who install solar panels, wind turbines, or other renewable energy systems in their homes.

Nonbusiness Energy Property Credit: This credit is available to homeowners who make energy-efficient improvements to their primary residences, such as installing energy-efficient windows or upgrading their heating and cooling systems.

Commercial Building Tax Deduction: This deduction is available to commercial building owners who make energy-efficient improvements to their properties, such as upgrading their lighting systems or installing more efficient HVAC systems.

Opportunity Zone Tax Benefits

Opportunity Zones are designated areas that are intended to encourage investment and economic growth in low-income communities. Real estate investors who invest in Opportunity Zones can take advantage of several tax benefits, including:

Deferral of capital gains taxes: Investors can defer paying capital gains taxes on the sale of an asset if they reinvest the proceeds in an Opportunity Zone within 180 days of the sale.

Reduction of capital gains taxes: If investors hold their Opportunity Zone investment for at least five years, they can reduce their capital gains tax liability by 10%. If they hold the investment for at least seven years, they can reduce their capital gains tax liability by an additional 5%.

Tax-free appreciation: If investors hold their Opportunity Zone investment for at least 10 years, they can sell the investment without paying any capital gains taxes on the appreciation.

Overall, tax credits can be a valuable tool for real estate investors who are looking to reduce their tax liability while also making a positive impact in their communities. However, it's important to consult with a tax professional to ensure that you're taking advantage of all of the tax credits and deductions that are available to you.

Risks and Rewards of Real Estate Investments

Investing in real estate can be an exciting and potentially lucrative opportunity for building wealth over time. However, like any investment, there are both risks and rewards associated with investing in real estate.

In this chapter, we will explore the risks and rewards of investing in real estate, so you can make an informed decision when considering whether or not to invest in this asset class.

Risks of Real Estate Investments

Market Risk

One of the primary risks associated with investing in real estate is market risk. This risk involves the possibility of a decline in property values, which can occur due to factors such as changes in interest rates, economic conditions, or local market conditions.

Market risk can be mitigated by investing in properties with stable demand, such as those located in desirable neighborhoods or with unique features that set them apart from the competition.

Liquidity Risk

Real estate investments are considered relatively illiquid, meaning they cannot be easily sold or converted to cash. Unlike stocks or other financial investments, real estate investments can take time to sell, and the process can be complicated and costly.

To mitigate liquidity risk, it's essential to consider your investment timeline and liquidity needs before investing in real estate. You may want to diversify your portfolio with other assets that offer greater liquidity, such as stocks or bonds.

Management Risk

Real estate investments require active management, which can be time-consuming and require specialized knowledge and expertise. Without proper management, properties can quickly deteriorate, and their value can decline.

To mitigate management risk, consider hiring a professional property management company to oversee your properties. This can help ensure that your investment properties are well-maintained, and tenant issues are handled efficiently.

Financing Risk

Financing real estate investments can be risky, particularly if you take on too much debt. If you're unable to make mortgage payments or interest rates rise, you could face foreclosure and lose your investment.

To mitigate financing risk, consider investing in properties that generate enough cash flow to cover mortgage payments and other expenses. It's also essential to have a solid financial plan in place and to have an emergency fund to cover unexpected expenses.

Rewards of Real Estate Investments

Cash Flow

One of the primary benefits of investing in real estate is the potential for generating steady cash flow. Rental income from investment properties can provide a steady stream of passive income, which can help you achieve financial independence and build wealth over time.

To maximize cash flow, it's important to invest in properties that generate high rental yields relative to their purchase price. This can involve selecting properties in high-demand areas or with unique features that command premium rental rates.

Appreciation

Another potential benefit of investing in real estate is the potential for long-term appreciation in property values. While property values can be volatile in the short term, over the long term, real estate values tend to appreciate at a relatively stable rate.

To maximize appreciation potential, it's essential to invest in properties with strong fundamentals, such as those located in high-demand areas, with good schools, and proximity to transportation and other amenities.

Tax Benefits

Real estate investments offer several tax benefits that can help reduce your tax liability and increase your after-tax returns. These benefits include depreciation deductions, property tax deductions, and mortgage interest deductions.

To maximize tax benefits, it's essential to work with a knowledgeable tax professional who can help you identify all available deductions and ensure that you're in compliance with all relevant tax laws and regulations.

Diversification

Investing in real estate can offer diversification benefits to a portfolio. Real estate investments often have low correlation with other asset classes, such as stocks or bonds, which means they can help to reduce overall portfolio volatility and potentially improve returns.

To maximize diversification benefits, consider investing in a mix of different types of real estate, such as residential, commercial, industrial, and retail properties. Additionally, consider diversifying geographically, investing in properties located in different regions or even different countries.

Strategies for Real Estate Investments

Investing in real estate requires careful planning and execution. Some key strategies for successful real estate investing include:

Conduct thorough research: Before investing in any real estate property, it's important to conduct a thorough analysis of the local real estate market, the property itself, and the financial and legal implications of the investment.

Develop a sound investment plan: A solid investment plan should include a detailed financial plan, marketing and tenant acquisition strategies, and plans for property management and maintenance.

Diversify your portfolio: To maximize the potential rewards of real estate investing and minimize the risks, consider diversifying your portfolio by investing in a mix of different types of real estate and geographies.

Stay up-to-date with market trends: Real estate investing is a dynamic field, and it's important to stay up-to-date with the latest market trends and developments to make informed investment decisions.

Work with experienced professionals: Real estate investing can be complex, and it's important to work with experienced professionals, such as real estate agents, property managers, and attorneys, to ensure that your investments are structured and managed effectively.

Conclusion

Investing in real estate can be a rewarding way to build wealth over the long-term, but it also comes with risks. By understanding both the risks and rewards of real estate investing and implementing sound investment strategies, investors can increase their chances of success.

To recap, some of the key takeaways from this chapter include:

Real estate investing can offer potentially high returns, but it also comes with risks, such as property value fluctuations, rental income fluctuations, and unforeseen expenses.

Understanding the risks and rewards of real estate investing is essential for making informed investment decisions.

Some of the potential rewards of real estate investing include cash flow from rental income, long-term capital appreciation, tax benefits, and portfolio diversification.

There are various ways to invest in real estate, including buying physical properties, investing in REITs, crowdfunding, and private equity funds.

Different types of real estate investments have different risks and rewards, so it's important to do your research and choose an investment strategy that aligns with your goals and risk tolerance.

Strategies for managing risk in real estate investing include conducting thorough research, developing a solid investment plan, diversifying your portfolio, and maintaining adequate liquidity.

Real estate investing can be complex and requires a significant amount of knowledge and experience. It's important to consult with financial and legal professionals to ensure that you are making informed decisions and complying with all applicable laws and regulations.

In conclusion, real estate investing can be a lucrative way to build wealth over the long-term, but it's not without its risks. By understanding the risks and rewards of real estate investing, and implementing sound investment strategies, investors can increase their chances of success and achieve their financial goals.

Strategies for Investing in Real Estate in detail

Real estate investing can offer a variety of opportunities to build wealth and achieve financial goals, but there is no one-size-fits-all strategy for investing in this asset class. The best strategy for investing in real estate will depend on an investor's goals, risk tolerance, investment experience, and available resources. In this chapter, we will discuss some of the most common strategies for investing in real estate, including both active and passive investment strategies.

Buy and Hold Strategy

The buy and hold strategy is a popular real estate investment strategy that involves purchasing a property with the intention of holding onto it for an extended period of time, usually several years or even decades. The primary goal of this strategy is to generate passive income through rental income, while also benefiting from long-term appreciation in the value of the property. This strategy is well-suited for investors who are seeking a long-term investment with relatively stable returns and a low level of risk.

One advantage of the buy and hold strategy is that it allows investors to build equity over time, as the value of the property increases and the mortgage balance decreases. This can create opportunities for refinancing or selling the property for a profit in the future. Another advantage is that this strategy can provide steady cash flow, particularly in markets with high demand for rental properties.

House Hacking

House hacking is a strategy that involves purchasing a multi-unit property, such as a duplex or triplex, and living in one of the units while renting out the others. This strategy can help investors to offset the cost of their mortgage and other expenses by generating rental income from the other units. House hacking can be an excellent way for first-time investors to get started in real estate investing, as it can help to minimize the cost of living expenses while building equity and generating income.

One of the primary advantages of house hacking is that it can offer a relatively low-risk way to get started in real estate investing, particularly if the investor is able to secure a favorable mortgage rate. Additionally, house hacking can provide a variety of tax benefits, including deductions for mortgage interest, property taxes, and other expenses.

Flipping

Flipping is a real estate investment strategy that involves purchasing a property with the intention of renovating it and then selling it for a profit. This strategy is typically used by more experienced investors who are comfortable taking on higher levels of risk, as it can involve significant upfront costs and requires a good understanding of the local real estate market and renovation costs.

One of the primary advantages of flipping is that it can offer potentially high returns in a relatively short period of time. Successful flippers can purchase properties at a discount, make strategic renovations, and sell them for a profit in a matter of months. However, flipping also comes with significant risks, including the risk of overestimating the value of the property or underestimating renovation costs.

Real Estate Investment Trusts (REITs)

Real Estate Investment Trusts, or REITs, are a type of passive real estate investment that allows investors to pool their money together to invest in a portfolio of income-generating real estate assets. REITs are publicly traded, which means they can be bought and sold on stock exchanges, making them a relatively easy and accessible way for investors to invest in real estate.

One of the primary advantages of REITs is that they offer the potential for regular income through dividends, as well as the opportunity for long-term appreciation in the value of the underlying real estate assets. Additionally, REITs offer a level of liquidity that is not typically available with other types of real estate investments, as they can be bought and sold on stock exchanges.

Real Estate Crowdfunding

Real Estate Crowdfunding is a relatively new and increasingly popular way to invest in real estate. Crowdfunding platforms allow investors to pool their funds to invest in real estate projects. These platforms offer various types of investments, ranging from debt to equity, and offer different minimum investment amounts.

One of the main benefits of real estate crowdfunding is the ability to access real estate investment opportunities with a lower minimum investment requirement than traditional real estate investing. This allows investors with smaller budgets to diversify their portfolio and invest in a variety of projects.

However, as with any investment, there are also risks associated with real estate crowdfunding. It's important for investors to thoroughly research the platform and the investment opportunity before committing funds. Additionally, real estate crowdfunding investments are typically illiquid, meaning that it may be difficult to sell an investment before its maturity date.

Real Estate Partnerships

Another way to invest in real estate is through partnerships. Real estate partnerships involve multiple investors pooling their resources to purchase a property. These partnerships are typically structured as Limited Liability Companies (LLCs) or Limited Partnerships (LPs).

One of the advantages of real estate partnerships is the ability to diversify investment risk by spreading funds across multiple properties. Partnerships can also provide access to larger and more complex real estate deals that individual investors may not be able to finance on their own.

However, investing in real estate partnerships comes with some risks. One of the primary risks is the possibility of disagreements among partners, which can result in delays or even the termination of the partnership. Additionally, real estate partnerships can be illiquid, meaning that it may be difficult to sell a partnership interest before the property is sold.

Real Estate Investment Trusts (REITs), real estate crowdfunding, and real estate partnerships are just a few examples of the many ways to invest in real estate. Each strategy comes with its own risks and rewards, and it's important for investors to do their due diligence and carefully consider their options before committing funds. With proper research and a sound investment plan, real estate investing can be a lucrative way to build wealth over the long term.

In conclusion, investing in real estate can be a viable way to build wealth and achieve financial freedom over the long-term. Whether you're investing in residential, commercial, industrial, retail, or mixed-use properties, it's important to do your due diligence, develop a sound investment plan, and consider the potential risks and rewards of your chosen investment strategy.

Financing your real estate investments is also an important consideration, as there are a variety of financing options available depending on your financial situation and investment goals. Taking advantage of the tax benefits associated with real estate investing can also help to maximize your returns and minimize your tax liability.

Ultimately, successful real estate investing requires a combination of research, planning, and execution. By staying informed about the latest trends and strategies in real estate investing, and working with trusted professionals such as real estate agents, attorneys, and financial advisors, you can increase your chances of achieving your financial goals and building a strong, diversified real estate portfolio.

CHAPTER 7 - REAL ESTATE MARKET ANALYSIS

- ❖ Understanding the Real Estate Market
- ❖ Market Trends
- ❖ Factors that Affect Real Estate Prices
- ❖ Real Estate Market Indicators
- ❖ Analyzing Real Estate Data

Real estate investing requires a deep understanding of the market and the factors that drive property values. Before investing in a property, it's important to conduct a thorough analysis of the local real estate market to determine if it's the right time and place to invest.

Market analysis is an essential part of real estate investing, whether you're a seasoned investor or just starting out. By understanding the market, you can identify opportunities and risks, and make informed decisions that can help you achieve your investment goals.

In this chapter, we'll explore the key factors to consider when conducting a real estate market analysis, including supply and demand, economic indicators, and local market conditions. We'll also discuss the tools and resources available to help you conduct a comprehensive market analysis and make informed investment decisions.

Understanding the Real Estate Market

Understanding the real estate market is an essential part of successful real estate investing. By analyzing trends, market conditions, and economic factors, investors can make informed decisions that can help maximize their returns and mitigate risks.

In this chapter, we'll explore the key concepts and factors that go into understanding the real estate market. From supply and demand to economic indicators and local market conditions, we'll cover the most important considerations that real estate investors need to keep in mind.

Supply and Demand

Like any market, the real estate market is driven by the forces of supply and demand. When there is high demand for real estate but a limited supply, prices tend to rise. Conversely, when supply exceeds demand, prices tend to fall.

In order to understand the supply and demand dynamics of the real estate market, it's important to consider a variety of factors. These can include the number of available properties, the amount of new construction, and the overall health of the local economy.

For example, if there is a growing population in a particular area but a limited supply of housing, demand for real estate is likely to be high. This can lead to increased competition for available properties, which in turn can drive up prices.

On the other hand, if there is a surplus of properties and a low level of demand, sellers may be forced to lower their prices in order to attract buyers. This can create opportunities for investors to find bargains and potentially generate high returns on their investments.

Economic Indicators

In addition to supply and demand, the real estate market is also influenced by a wide range of economic indicators. These can include factors such as interest rates, inflation, unemployment, and GDP growth.

Interest rates are a particularly important economic indicator for real estate investors, as they can have a significant impact on the cost of financing real estate investments. When interest rates are low, borrowing costs are generally lower, making it more affordable to invest in real estate. Conversely, when interest rates are high, financing costs can be much more expensive, which can make it more difficult to generate positive returns on investments.

Inflation is another economic factor that can have an impact on the real estate market. When inflation is high, the value of the currency tends to decline, which can lead to higher prices for goods and services. This can include real estate prices, as sellers may demand higher prices in order to offset the declining value of the currency. Conversely, when inflation is low, prices may be more stable and predictable.

Other economic indicators, such as GDP growth and unemployment rates, can also provide important insights into the health of the real estate market. When the economy is growing and unemployment rates are low, it tends to create a positive environment for real estate investing, as more people have the financial means to purchase properties.

Local Market Conditions

Finally, it's important to consider the local market conditions when investing in real estate. This can include factors such as local zoning laws, property taxes, and the overall economic health of the region.

By understanding the local market conditions, investors can identify opportunities to invest in properties that are likely to appreciate in value over time. For example, if a particular area is experiencing strong economic growth and rising property values, it may be a good time to invest in real estate in that area.

Likewise, if a particular region is struggling with high unemployment rates and stagnant economic growth, it may not be the best time to invest in real estate in that area.

Conclusion

Understanding the real estate market is a crucial component of successful real estate investing. By analyzing supply and demand dynamics, economic indicators, and local market conditions, investors can make informed decisions that can help maximize their returns and mitigate risks. Whether you are a seasoned real estate investor or just getting started, taking the time to understand the real estate market can help you make the most of your investments.

Keep in mind that real estate market conditions can change quickly, so it's important to regularly monitor trends and adjust your strategy as needed. Additionally, real estate market analysis is just one piece of the puzzle when it comes to successful real estate investing. It's also important to have a solid investment plan in place, understand financing options, and carefully consider the risks and rewards of each potential investment.

Overall, a strong understanding of the real estate market can give investors a competitive edge and increase their chances of success in the world of real estate investing. By staying informed and being diligent in their research and analysis, investors can make informed decisions that can lead to long-term financial stability and growth.

Market Trends

Market trends can have a significant impact on the real estate industry. By understanding these trends, investors can gain valuable insights into the direction of the market and make informed decisions about their real estate investments.

One important market trend to consider is the state of the economy. The overall health of the economy can have a major impact on the real estate market, as it affects factors such as interest rates, job growth, and consumer spending. For example, a strong economy may lead to increased demand for real estate as people have more money to spend and are more confident in their financial futures. On the other hand, a weak economy may lead to decreased demand for real estate as people cut back on spending and are more cautious about making major purchases.

Another market trend to consider is the level of housing supply and demand. This can vary greatly depending on the location and type of property. In areas with a high demand for housing and a limited supply, prices may rise as buyers compete for available properties. In areas with an oversupply of housing, prices may fall as sellers compete for buyers.

Demographic trends are also important to consider when analyzing the real estate market. For example, the aging of the baby boomer generation has led to an increased demand for retirement communities and assisted living facilities. Similarly, the rise of the millennial generation has led to increased demand for affordable housing, particularly in urban areas.

Technology is another factor that can have a major impact on the real estate market. Advances in technology have made it easier for buyers and sellers to connect, with many transactions now taking place online. This has led to an increase in transparency and efficiency in the real estate market, as well as the rise of new business models such as real estate crowdfunding.

Environmental factors can also play a role in the real estate market. For example, areas that are prone to natural disasters such as hurricanes or wildfires may see decreased demand for real estate, as buyers are more cautious about purchasing properties in these areas. On the other hand, areas that are seen as environmentally friendly, such as those with strong recycling programs or a high number of LEED-certified buildings, may see increased demand for real estate as buyers become more environmentally conscious.

Overall, understanding market trends is a key component of successful real estate investing. By keeping an eye on economic indicators, supply and demand dynamics, demographic trends, technology, and environmental factors, investors can make informed decisions about when and where to invest in real estate.

Factors that Affect Real Estate Prices

As a real estate investor, it's important to understand the various factors that can affect real estate prices. By understanding these factors, you can make informed decisions when buying or selling real estate and maximize your returns. In this chapter, we will explore the main factors that influence real estate prices.

Location

The most important factor that affects real estate prices is location. Properties that are located in desirable areas with good schools, access to transportation, and amenities such as shopping and entertainment are in high demand and can command higher prices. On the other hand, properties that are located in less desirable areas, such as high-crime areas or areas with limited access to amenities, may be priced lower.

Supply and Demand

Supply and demand is another key factor that affects real estate prices. When there is high demand for properties in a certain area but a limited supply, prices are likely to go up. Conversely, when there is an oversupply of properties in an area and not enough buyers, prices may go down.

Economic Conditions

The overall economic conditions of a region or country can also impact real estate prices. In a strong economy with low unemployment and high consumer confidence, real estate prices are likely to go up. In a weak economy with high unemployment and low consumer confidence, real estate prices may decline.

Interest Rates

Interest rates also play a role in real estate prices. When interest rates are low, it is easier for buyers to secure mortgages, which can lead to increased demand and higher prices. On the other hand, when interest rates are high, buyers may be less likely to take out mortgages, leading to decreased demand and lower prices.

Demographics

Demographics can also have an impact on real estate prices. For example, as the baby boomer generation ages and enters retirement, demand for smaller, low-maintenance properties such as condos may increase, while demand for larger family homes may decline.

Infrastructure

The availability and quality of infrastructure such as roads, public transportation, and utilities can also impact real estate prices. Properties that are located in areas with good infrastructure are typically more desirable and can command higher prices.

Zoning and Land Use

Zoning and land use regulations can also affect real estate prices. For example, properties that are zoned for commercial use may be priced higher than those zoned for residential use. Similarly, properties that are located in areas with strict zoning laws and limited land use may be priced higher due to limited supply.

Property Condition and Amenities

Finally, the condition of the property itself and the amenities it offers can also impact real estate prices. Properties that are well-maintained and offer desirable features such as updated kitchens and bathrooms, outdoor living spaces, and energy-efficient features are typically more valuable and can command higher prices.

In conclusion, understanding the various factors that affect real estate prices is critical for successful real estate investing. By analyzing these factors and staying up to date on market trends, investors can make informed decisions and maximize their returns.

Real Estate Market Indicators

Real estate market indicators are data points that provide insight into the current state of the real estate market. By analyzing these indicators, investors can make informed decisions about buying, selling, or holding real estate investments. In this chapter, we will explore some of the most important real estate market indicators and how they can be used to gauge the health of the market.

Home Sales

One of the most basic indicators of the real estate market is home sales. Home sales data is typically reported on a monthly basis and includes the number of homes sold, the average sale price, and the median sale price. This data can provide insight into the demand for housing in a particular market and the level of competition among buyers.

Housing Inventory

Housing inventory refers to the number of homes available for sale in a particular market. Low inventory levels can indicate high demand and a competitive market, while high inventory levels may suggest a slower market with less competition among buyers.

Days on Market

Days on market (DOM) is a metric that measures the number of days it takes for a home to sell after it is listed on the market. This metric can be used to gauge the level of competition among buyers in a particular market. A low DOM indicates a high level of competition and a strong demand for housing.

Home Prices

Home prices are another important indicator of the real estate market. Home prices can provide insight into the level of demand for housing in a particular market, as well as the level of competition among buyers. In general, rising home prices suggest a strong demand for housing and a competitive market, while falling prices may indicate a slower market with less competition among buyers.

Mortgage Rates

Mortgage rates can have a significant impact on the real estate market. When mortgage rates are low, more people are able to afford to buy a home, which can increase demand and drive up prices.

Conversely, when mortgage rates are high, fewer people may be able to afford to buy a home, which can decrease demand and drive down prices.

Housing Starts

Housing starts refer to the number of new residential construction projects that have started in a particular market. This data can provide insight into the level of supply in a particular market. When housing starts are high, it can indicate a healthy real estate market with strong demand. However, when housing starts are low, it may suggest a slower market with less demand.

Foreclosure Rates

Foreclosure rates refer to the number of homes in a particular market that are in the process of foreclosure. High foreclosure rates can indicate a distressed market with an oversupply of homes. This data can be used to identify markets that may present good investment opportunities.

Rental Rates

Rental rates can provide insight into the level of demand for rental properties in a particular market. When rental rates are high, it can suggest a strong demand for rental properties and a competitive market. Conversely, when rental rates are low, it may indicate a slower market with less demand.

Population Growth

Population growth is an important indicator of the real estate market, as it can affect the level of demand for housing in a particular market. When population growth is high, it can indicate a strong demand for housing and a competitive market. However, when population growth is low, it may suggest a slower market with less demand.

Economic Indicators

Economic indicators such as GDP growth, employment rates, and consumer confidence can also have an impact on the real estate market. When the economy is strong and consumer confidence is high, it can indicate a healthy real estate market with strong demand. Conversely, when the economy is weak and consumer confidence is low, it may suggest a slower market with less demand.

In conclusion, understanding real estate market indicators is a key component of successful real estate investing. By keeping track of important indicators, investors can make informed decisions that can help maximize their returns and mitigate risks. It's important to note that no single indicator should be relied upon in isolation, and that investors should look at a range of indicators to get a well-rounded view of the market.

Whether you're a seasoned real estate investor or just getting started, taking the time to understand real estate market indicators can help you make more informed investment decisions. By paying attention to the supply and demand dynamics in a given market, tracking economic indicators, and monitoring local market conditions, you can better position yourself to make smart real estate investments. Remember to stay up to date with changes in the market, and to regularly re-evaluate your investment strategy to ensure that you are making the most of your opportunities.

Analyzing Real Estate Data

Real estate investing requires a great deal of research and analysis to make informed decisions. Analyzing real estate data is a critical component of the investment process. With the increasing availability of data, real estate investors have more tools than ever before to help them make informed decisions. In this chapter, we will discuss the different types of real estate data that are available and how to use them to make informed investment decisions.

Types of Real Estate Data

There are many types of real estate data available that can help investors make informed decisions. Here are some of the most common types of real estate data:

Market Data: Market data includes information on current and historical sales, rental rates, and occupancy rates. This data can be used to evaluate supply and demand dynamics, identify trends in the market, and determine the fair market value of a property.

Demographic Data: Demographic data includes information on the population, age, income, education level, and other characteristics of a given area. This data can be used to evaluate the potential demand for a property, identify target markets, and determine the appropriate marketing strategies.

Economic Data: Economic data includes information on factors such as interest rates, unemployment rates, GDP, and inflation rates. This data can be used to evaluate the overall health of the economy, identify potential risks or opportunities, and determine the appropriate investment strategies.

Property Data: Property data includes information on specific properties, such as their size, age, condition, and amenities. This data can be used to evaluate the potential return on investment, identify any potential issues or risks, and determine the appropriate offer price.

Real Estate Investment Trust (REIT) Data: REIT data includes information on the performance of publicly traded real estate investment trusts. This data can be used to evaluate the performance of different types of real estate assets, identify trends in the market, and determine the appropriate investment strategies.

How to Analyze Real Estate Data

Analyzing real estate data can be a complex process. However, with the right tools and techniques, investors can make informed decisions that can help maximize their returns and mitigate risks. Here are some steps to follow when analyzing real estate data:

Identify the Relevant Data: Start by identifying the types of real estate data that are relevant to your investment decision. Consider the location, type of property, target market, and investment goals when determining what types of data to analyze.

Collect the Data: Once you have identified the relevant data, you will need to collect it. There are many sources of real estate data, including public records, online databases, and real estate professionals. Consider the reliability and accuracy of the data when collecting it.

Clean and Organize the Data: Real estate data can be messy and disorganized. To make it usable, you will need to clean and organize it. This may involve removing duplicates, filling in missing data, and standardizing formats.

Analyze the Data: Once the data is cleaned and organized, you can start to analyze it. This may involve calculating averages, identifying trends, and creating visualizations to help you better understand the data.

Make Informed Decisions: The ultimate goal of analyzing real estate data is to make informed investment decisions. Use the data to identify potential risks and opportunities, evaluate the potential return on investment, and determine the appropriate investment strategies.

Tools for Analyzing Real Estate Data

There are many tools available to help real estate investors analyze data. Here are some of the most common tools:

Spreadsheets: Spreadsheets, such as Microsoft Excel or Google Sheets, can be used to organize and analyze real estate data. They can also be used to create visualizations, such as charts or graphs.

Real Estate Investment Real estate investment software can be a powerful tool for analyzing and managing real estate data. These programs can provide investors with a wide range of features, such as property analysis tools, financial modeling, and portfolio management.

One popular type of real estate investment software is real estate investment analysis (REIA) software. This software can help investors analyze the financial viability of potential real estate investments by creating detailed reports and projections based on a range of variables.

Another type of real estate investment software is property management software. This type of software is designed to help real estate investors manage and track their property portfolios, including tenant management, lease tracking, and financial reporting.

Real Estate Analytics

Real estate analytics refers to the use of data analysis and statistics to understand real estate markets and make informed investment decisions. Real estate analytics can encompass a wide range of techniques and tools, including data mining, machine learning, and predictive analytics.

One common application of real estate analytics is in market analysis. By analyzing data on property values, rents, and other economic indicators, investors can gain insights into market trends and potential investment opportunities.

Real estate analytics can also be used to analyze property performance, such as by tracking occupancy rates, rental income, and other financial metrics. By using real estate analytics tools and techniques, investors can gain a deeper understanding of their real estate portfolios and make more informed decisions about buying, selling, or holding properties.

Real Estate Marketplaces

Real estate marketplaces, such as Zillow, Redfin, or Realtor.com, can be a valuable resource for real estate investors looking to research potential investment properties. These marketplaces typically offer a wide range of tools and resources for real estate buyers and sellers, including property listings, market data, and neighborhood information.

One of the primary benefits of real estate marketplaces is that they can provide investors with real-time access to property listings and pricing information. This can be especially useful for investors who are looking to move quickly on investment opportunities or who are looking to keep track of market trends in specific regions or neighborhoods.

Real estate marketplaces can also be a valuable source of data and insights on local real estate markets. By analyzing data on property values, rental rates, and other economic indicators, investors can gain a better understanding of market trends and identify potential investment opportunities.

Conclusion

Analyzing real estate data is a critical component of successful real estate investing. By understanding the various tools and techniques for analyzing real estate data, investors can gain insights into market trends, identify potential investment opportunities, and make informed decisions about buying, selling, or holding properties. Whether you are a seasoned real estate investor or just starting out, taking the time to understand real estate data analysis can help you make the most of your investments and achieve your financial goals.

In conclusion, understanding the real estate market is a critical factor in successful real estate investing. By analyzing various market indicators, such as supply and demand, economic trends, and local market conditions, investors can make informed decisions that can help them maximize their returns and minimize their risks.

Real estate market analysis is a constantly evolving process that requires investors to stay up to date on the latest trends and indicators. Fortunately, with the advent of technology and the wealth of data available, investors have access to more information than ever before. By leveraging this information and using the appropriate tools to analyze real estate data, investors can make more informed decisions that can lead to greater success.

Ultimately, successful real estate investing requires a combination of market knowledge, financial expertise, and a willingness to adapt to changing market conditions. By taking the time to understand the real estate market and developing a sound investment strategy, investors can achieve their financial goals and build long-term wealth through real estate.

CHAPTER 8 - REAL ESTATE INVESTMENT RISKS AND CHALLENGES

- ❖ Real Estate Market Fluctuations
- ❖ Economic Factors
- ❖ Regulatory Risks
- ❖ Operational Risks
- ❖ Legal Risks

Real estate investing can be a lucrative way to build wealth and achieve financial independence. However, like any investment, it comes with inherent risks and challenges. Understanding these risks and challenges is key to making informed investment decisions and mitigating potential losses. In this chapter, we will explore some of the most significant risks and challenges that real estate investors may encounter.

Real Estate Market Fluctuations

Real estate markets are cyclical, and property values can fluctuate rapidly due to changes in supply and demand, interest rates, and economic conditions. When property values decline, investors may experience a decrease in the value of their investment, making it difficult to sell the property or refinance it.

One way to mitigate the risk of market fluctuations is to invest in properties that generate a stable and predictable cash flow. For example, rental properties that generate consistent rental income can provide a reliable source of income even during market downturns.

However, even stable rental income may not be enough to weather significant market fluctuations. In order to fully understand the risks associated with market fluctuations, it is important to have a clear understanding of how they occur, what causes them, and how they can be managed.

Real estate market fluctuations can be caused by a number of factors. Changes in interest rates, economic conditions, and supply and demand can all affect the value of properties. For example, when interest rates rise, it becomes more expensive for buyers to take out loans to purchase property. This can lead to a decrease in demand and a corresponding drop in property values.

Similarly, economic conditions can have a significant impact on real estate markets. When the economy is strong and job growth is high, demand for properties may increase, leading to higher property values. Conversely, during economic downturns or recessions, demand for properties may decrease, leading to lower property values.

Finally, supply and demand imbalances can also affect real estate market fluctuations. For example, if there is an oversupply of properties on the market, this can lead to decreased demand and lower property values. Alternatively, a shortage of properties can lead to increased demand and higher property values.

While it is impossible to completely eliminate the risk of market fluctuations, there are strategies that real estate investors can use to manage this risk. One approach is to diversify your real estate holdings across different markets, asset classes, and geographic regions. By doing so, you can reduce your exposure to any one particular market and spread your risk across a broader range of assets.

Another approach is to invest in properties that are likely to hold their value during market downturns. For example, properties in highly desirable locations with limited supply may be less affected by market fluctuations than properties in oversupplied or less desirable locations.

Real estate investors can also use financial instruments such as options, futures, and other derivatives to hedge against the risk of market fluctuations. These instruments allow investors to lock in prices for future transactions, providing a degree of protection against fluctuations in the market.

It is also important to keep in mind that market fluctuations are a normal part of the real estate market cycle. By taking a long-term approach to real estate investing and being patient during market downturns, investors may be able to realize significant gains over time.

In addition to these strategies, real estate investors can also stay informed about market trends and conditions by keeping up to date with industry news, economic data, and other relevant information. This can help investors make informed decisions about when to buy or sell properties, and when to adjust their investment strategies to manage risk.

Overall, market fluctuations are an inherent risk of real estate investing, but they can be managed through a combination of diversification, strategic property selection, and financial hedging strategies. By staying informed and being patient, real estate investors can navigate the ups and downs of the market and achieve long-term success in their investments.

Economic Factors

Economic factors can also impact the real estate market, including inflation, interest rates, and unemployment rates. When interest rates rise, it can become more expensive to finance real estate investments, potentially reducing the number of potential buyers and decreasing demand. Economic downturns can also lead to higher unemployment rates, which can decrease demand for housing and result in lower property values.

One way to mitigate the risk of economic factors is to invest in stable and diverse economies. Cities with strong job growth and diverse industries are less likely to experience significant downturns in the real estate market, providing investors with a more stable and predictable investment.

In addition, investors can also pay attention to macroeconomic indicators such as gross domestic product (GDP), consumer price index (CPI), and housing starts to gain insight into the health of the economy and potential impact on the real estate market. For example, a rising GDP can indicate a healthy economy with potential for job growth, while a high CPI can signal inflationary pressures that may lead to higher interest rates.

Another economic factor to consider is the supply and demand balance within the real estate market. When there is a surplus of available properties, sellers may be forced to lower prices in order to attract buyers. Conversely, in a market with limited inventory, sellers may be able to demand higher prices due to increased demand. Understanding the supply and demand dynamics within a particular market can help investors make informed decisions about when to buy or sell real estate.

Another economic factor that can affect real estate investments is tax policy. Changes in tax laws, such as the tax code revisions that took effect in 2018, can have significant implications for real estate investors. For example, the new tax laws limited the amount of deductions that can be taken for mortgage interest and state and local taxes, which may impact the affordability of owning a home in certain areas.

Real estate investors can also be impacted by broader economic factors, such as global economic conditions, trade policies, and geopolitical events. Economic instability in other countries, changes in trade policies, or political unrest can all have ripple effects throughout the global economy and impact the real estate market.

To mitigate the risk of economic factors, investors can work to diversify their real estate investments. By spreading investments across different asset classes and geographic regions, investors can reduce the impact of any one economic factor on their overall portfolio. Additionally, investors can stay informed about the economic climate and stay up to date on changes in tax policy, interest rates, and other economic indicators that may impact the real estate market.

Regulatory Risks

Real estate investors must comply with a variety of laws and regulations, including zoning laws, building codes, environmental regulations, and tenant laws. Failure to comply with these regulations can result in fines, lawsuits, and other legal consequences, potentially leading to significant financial losses.

One way to mitigate regulatory risks is to work with experienced real estate professionals, such as attorneys, accountants, and property managers, who can help investors navigate the complex legal landscape. It is also important to stay up to date on changes to local and national laws and regulations that may impact real estate investments.

Regulatory risks are a critical consideration for real estate investors, as non-compliance with various regulations can result in legal, financial, and reputational consequences. Real estate is a heavily regulated industry, and investors must comply with a wide range of laws and regulations at the local, state, and federal levels. Some of the most common regulatory risks that real estate investors face include zoning laws, building codes, environmental regulations, and tenant laws.

Zoning laws are a critical consideration for real estate investors, as they dictate how a property can be used and developed. Zoning laws vary by jurisdiction and can include restrictions on the type of structures that can be built, the maximum height and density of buildings, and the allowable uses of the property. Failure to comply with zoning laws can result in fines, legal action, and the loss of the property.

Building codes are another key regulatory consideration for real estate investors, as they dictate the standards for the design, construction, and safety of buildings. Building codes vary by jurisdiction and can include requirements for structural integrity, fire safety, plumbing, and electrical systems. Failure to comply with building codes can result in fines, legal action, and even the condemnation of the property.

Environmental regulations are another important consideration for real estate investors, particularly for those investing in commercial or industrial properties. Environmental regulations can include requirements for hazardous waste management, air and water quality, and the remediation of contaminated sites. Failure to comply with environmental regulations can result in fines, legal action, and reputational damage.

Tenant laws are also critical for real estate investors who own rental properties. Tenant laws vary by jurisdiction and can include requirements for habitability, rent control, and eviction procedures. Failure to comply with tenant laws can result in legal action, fines, and even the loss of the property.

To mitigate regulatory risks, real estate investors should work with experienced professionals, such as attorneys, accountants, and property managers. These professionals can help investors navigate the complex legal landscape, ensure compliance with various regulations, and mitigate the risk of legal action or financial penalties. It is also important to stay up to date on changes to local and national laws and regulations that may impact real estate investments.

Investors can also mitigate regulatory risks by conducting thorough due diligence before making a real estate investment. This includes researching zoning laws, building codes, environmental regulations, and tenant laws in the local area, as well as understanding any pending regulatory changes that may impact the investment. By taking a proactive approach to regulatory compliance, investors can mitigate the risk of legal, financial, and reputational consequences and ensure the long-term success of their real estate investments.

In conclusion, regulatory risks are a critical consideration for real estate investors, and failure to comply with various regulations can result in significant legal, financial, and reputational consequences. Real estate investors can mitigate regulatory risks by working with experienced professionals, conducting thorough due diligence, and staying up to date on changes to local and national laws and regulations. By taking a proactive approach to regulatory compliance, investors can maximize the success of their real estate investments and avoid costly legal and financial penalties.

Operational Risks

Owning and managing real estate can come with a variety of operational risks, including maintenance and repair costs, tenant turnover, and property damage. These risks can be exacerbated by factors such as natural disasters, economic downturns, and unexpected events.

One way to mitigate operational risks is to conduct regular property inspections and maintenance to identify and address issues before they become major problems. It is also important to have contingency plans in place to address unexpected events, such as loss of rental income due to a tenant's inability to pay rent.

Operational risks are inherent in owning and managing real estate. These risks can impact the profitability and viability of an investment, as well as the overall success of a real estate portfolio. It is essential for investors to understand the types of operational risks they may face and how to mitigate them to protect their investments.

One of the most common operational risks is maintenance and repair costs. Properties require ongoing maintenance and repairs to keep them in good condition and ensure that they remain attractive to tenants. However, unexpected maintenance issues can arise, such as plumbing or electrical problems, that can be costly to fix. Property owners must be prepared to handle these issues promptly and have the resources to cover the costs.

Another operational risk is tenant turnover. When tenants leave, it can be challenging to find new tenants, resulting in a loss of rental income. Property owners may also incur additional costs associated with finding and screening new tenants. To mitigate this risk, property owners should maintain strong relationships with existing tenants, provide excellent customer service, and keep rents competitive with market rates.

Property damage is another operational risk that can result in significant financial losses. Natural disasters, such as hurricanes, tornadoes, or floods, can cause severe damage to properties. Property owners must have insurance coverage to help cover the cost of repairs and losses due to tenant displacement. It is also essential to have an emergency plan in place to minimize damage and respond quickly in the event of a disaster.

Unexpected events, such as the COVID-19 pandemic, can also pose significant operational risks for real estate investors. The pandemic has caused significant disruptions to the real estate industry, including rental income losses and tenant eviction moratoriums. Property owners must be prepared to handle unexpected events and adjust their operations accordingly. This may involve diversifying their investment portfolios, leveraging technology, or adjusting their business models.

To mitigate operational risks, property owners should conduct regular property inspections to identify and address maintenance and repair issues promptly. Property owners should also have contingency plans in place for unexpected events, such as natural disasters or economic downturns. For example, having a cash reserve to cover unexpected expenses, such as repairs or lost rental income, can help property owners weather unexpected events.

Another way to mitigate operational risks is to work with professional property management companies. Property managers can handle day-to-day operations, such as maintenance requests and rent collection, and have experience dealing with unexpected events. This can help reduce the burden on property owners and ensure that properties are well-managed and well-maintained.

In conclusion, operational risks are an inherent part of real estate investing. Property owners must be prepared to handle a variety of challenges, such as maintenance and repair costs, tenant turnover, and property damage. To mitigate these risks, property owners should conduct regular property inspections, have contingency plans in place for unexpected events, and work with professional property management companies. By taking proactive measures, property owners can minimize the impact of operational risks on their real estate investments and help ensure their long-term success.

Legal Risks

Real estate investors may also face legal risks, including lawsuits from tenants, neighbors, or other parties. Legal risks can also arise from contract disputes, property liens, and other legal issues.

One way to mitigate legal risks is to have a comprehensive insurance policy that covers potential legal issues, such as liability insurance and errors and omissions insurance. It is also important to work with experienced real estate professionals, such as attorneys and property managers, who can help investors navigate potential legal risks and develop effective strategies to protect their investments.

There are several legal risks that real estate investors should be aware of, including:

Contract disputes: Real estate investors must navigate a complex web of contracts, including purchase agreements, lease agreements, and property management agreements. Disputes over the terms of these contracts can lead to costly legal battles that can damage an investor's reputation and financial stability.

Property liens: Liens can be placed on a property for a variety of reasons, including unpaid taxes or unpaid debts owed by the owner. If a lien is placed on a property, it can prevent an investor from selling the property or refinancing it, potentially leading to significant financial losses.

Compliance with local and federal laws: Real estate investors must comply with a variety of local and federal laws and regulations, including zoning laws, building codes, and tenant laws. Failure to comply with these laws can result in fines, lawsuits, and other legal consequences.

Tenant disputes: Disputes with tenants can arise over a variety of issues, including rent payments, property damage, and lease terms. These disputes can result in legal battles that can be costly and time-consuming.

Property damage: Natural disasters, accidents, and other events can cause property damage that can be expensive to repair. If the damage is caused by a tenant, the landlord may need to take legal action to recover the costs of the repairs.

To mitigate legal risks, real estate investors should take several steps, including:

Conduct thorough due diligence: Before investing in a property, it is important to conduct a thorough investigation of the property's history, including any past legal issues. This can help identify potential legal risks before they become major problems.

Work with experienced professionals: Real estate investors should work with experienced attorneys, property managers, and other professionals who can provide guidance on legal issues and help develop effective strategies to protect their investments.

Maintain proper documentation: Investors should maintain accurate and complete documentation of all transactions and interactions with tenants, contractors, and other parties. This can help protect them in the event of a legal dispute.

Carry adequate insurance: Investors should carry adequate insurance coverage, including liability insurance, errors and omissions insurance, and property insurance, to protect against potential legal risks.

Develop contingency plans: Investors should develop contingency plans to address unexpected legal issues, such as tenant disputes or property damage. This can help minimize the financial and reputational damage that can result from legal disputes.

In conclusion, legal risks are a significant concern for real estate investors. By working with experienced professionals, maintaining proper documentation, and carrying adequate insurance, investors can mitigate the risk of legal issues and protect their investments. Conducting thorough due diligence and developing contingency plans can also help minimize the impact of unexpected legal issues.

Conclusion

Real estate investment can be a profitable and rewarding way to build wealth and achieve financial independence. However, like any investment, it comes with inherent risks and challenges. Understanding these risks and challenges is essential to making informed investment decisions and mitigating potential losses. By taking a thoughtful and strategic approach to real estate investing and working with experienced professionals, investors can minimize their risks and maximize their returns.

Real estate investment can be a lucrative opportunity for those who are willing to put in the work and make informed decisions. In order to be successful, investors must understand the key factors that impact real estate prices and values, as well as the risks and challenges that come with investing in this market.

In Chapter 4, we discussed the importance of location and the factors that make certain areas more desirable for real estate investment. By understanding local market conditions and analyzing supply and demand, investors can make informed decisions about where to invest their money.

Chapter 5 covered financing options for real estate investment, including traditional bank loans, private loans, and hard money loans. By carefully considering the pros and cons of each option, investors can choose the financing that best fits their individual needs and goals.

In Chapter 6, we explored the importance of analyzing real estate data in order to make informed decisions about investment opportunities. By using tools such as spreadsheets and real estate market indicators, investors can gain valuable insights into market trends and make better decisions.

Chapter 7 covered the risks associated with real estate investment, including market fluctuations, economic factors, regulatory risks, operational risks, and legal risks. By understanding these risks and taking steps to mitigate them, investors can better protect their investments.

Finally, in Chapter 8, we discussed the importance of property management and tenant relations. By maintaining a well-managed property and building positive relationships with tenants, investors can improve the profitability of their investments and reduce potential legal risks.

Overall, successful real estate investment requires a deep understanding of the market, as well as a willingness to take calculated risks and make informed decisions. By following the strategies and techniques outlined in these chapters, investors can build a profitable real estate portfolio that can provide long-term financial stability and growth.

PART 3
BLOCKCHAIN
INVESTING

CHAPTER 9 - A BRIEF HISTORY OF MONEY

What is Money?
The History of Money
The Evolution of Currency
The Role of Money in Society
The Future of Money

Money is an essential part of modern society, serving as a medium of exchange, a unit of account, and a store of value. While we often take money for granted in our daily lives, its history and evolution are fascinating and have played a significant role in shaping the world we live in today.

The history of money can be traced back to ancient times when people used bartering as a means of exchange. Bartering involves exchanging goods or services directly with one another without using money as an intermediary. However, bartering has its limitations, as it requires a double coincidence of wants between two parties for an exchange to take place.

To overcome the limitations of bartering, societies developed various forms of currency over time. The first known currency was created in ancient Mesopotamia in the form of clay tablets, which were used as a record of debt between individuals. Later, the Chinese began using cowry shells as a form of currency, and the first metal coins were minted in Lydia around 600 BCE.

Throughout history, various forms of currency have been used, including paper money, coins, and digital currencies. The evolution of currency has been shaped by advances in technology, economic development, and changes in social and political systems.

Money has played a critical role in shaping the world we live in today. It has enabled trade and commerce, promoted economic growth and development, and facilitated the exchange of goods and services across different countries and cultures. As such, money has had a profound impact on the way people live their lives, work, and interact with one another.

The future of money is also an area of ongoing debate and discussion. The rise of digital currencies such as Bitcoin and other cryptocurrencies has challenged traditional forms of currency and created new opportunities for investment and financial innovation. As technology continues to evolve, it is likely that new forms of currency will emerge, and the way we think about money and its role in society will continue to change.

In the following chapters, we will explore the evolution of currency in more detail and examine how it has shaped the world we live in today. We will also delve into the world of digital currencies and explore the potential opportunities and challenges they present for investors and society as a whole.

What is Money?

Money is a medium of exchange that facilitates the exchange of goods and services. It has been used by humans for thousands of years, and has taken many different forms throughout history.

At its core, money is a tool that allows people to trade goods and services without the need for a barter system. Instead of having to directly exchange goods, money serves as an intermediary that represents value and can be used to purchase goods or services.

One of the key characteristics of money is that it is widely accepted and recognized as a means of exchange. Without widespread acceptance, money loses its value and usefulness as a medium of exchange. For example, if someone were to try to use a currency that is not recognized or widely accepted, they would have a difficult time buying goods or services.

Money also serves as a store of value, meaning it can be saved and used at a later time. This characteristic allows people to save their money and use it to purchase goods or services in the future, providing a sense of security and stability.

In addition to its use as a medium of exchange and a store of value, money also serves as a unit of account. This means that it provides a common way to measure the value of goods and services, making it easier to compare prices and assess the value of different goods or services.

Money can take many different forms, from physical objects like gold and silver to digital currencies like Bitcoin. The history of money is a long and complex one, with many different forms of money being used throughout history.

Despite the different forms that money has taken, it has remained an essential part of human society, facilitating trade and exchange, providing a means of storing value, and serving as a unit of account. The evolution of money has been shaped by technological advances, economic developments, and social changes, and will continue to evolve in the future.

The History of Money

The history of money is a long and complex one, spanning thousands of years and multiple cultures. From the earliest forms of bartering to modern digital currencies, money has played a vital role in facilitating trade and commerce, enabling individuals and societies to acquire the goods and services they need to survive and thrive.

Early Forms of Currency

The earliest forms of currency were likely simple bartering systems, in which goods and services were exchanged directly for other goods and services. For example, a farmer might trade some of their crops for a cow from a rancher. While bartering systems were relatively simple and straightforward, they were also limited in terms of the types of goods and services that could be exchanged.

As societies became more complex and trade expanded beyond local communities, new forms of currency began to emerge. Some of the earliest examples of currency include cowry shells, which were used in various parts of the world as a form of currency, and metal coins, which were first introduced in China around 1000 BCE.

Coins quickly became popular in other parts of the world as well, and were eventually adopted by the Greeks and Romans as a standardized form of currency. The use of coins made it easier to conduct trade and commerce across long distances, and enabled individuals and societies to accumulate wealth and assets more easily.

Paper Money and Banknotes

The use of paper money and banknotes emerged in China during the Tang Dynasty, around the 7th century. Paper money was initially used as a form of promissory note, allowing individuals to exchange goods and services with the promise of payment at a later date. Eventually, paper money evolved into a standardized form of currency, with the first paper banknotes being issued in Sweden in the 17th century.

As the use of paper money became more widespread, it became easier to conduct large-scale trade and commerce across long distances, further facilitating economic growth and development. Today, paper money is still widely used around the world, with different countries issuing their own unique currencies.

Digital Currencies

In recent years, the rise of digital technologies has led to the emergence of new forms of currency, known as digital currencies. These currencies, which are often based on blockchain technology, allow for decentralized, peer-to-peer transactions that are not controlled by any central authority.

Bitcoin, the world's first and most well-known digital currency, was created in 2009 by an anonymous individual or group using the pseudonym Satoshi Nakamoto. Since then, thousands of other digital currencies, known as cryptocurrencies, have been created, with some of the most popular including Ethereum, Litecoin, and Ripple.

While digital currencies are still relatively new and often subject to volatility, they offer a number of potential benefits over traditional forms of currency, including lower transaction fees, increased security, and greater transparency.

Conclusion

The history of money is a long and complex one, marked by the evolution of various forms of currency, from bartering to paper money to digital currencies. While the specific forms of currency have changed over time, the role of money in facilitating trade and commerce has remained a constant throughout human history. As new forms of currency continue to emerge and evolve, it will be interesting to see how they impact the global economy and our daily lives.

The Evolution of Currency

The concept of currency has evolved over time, from bartering and trading goods and services to the development of physical currencies and the more recent emergence of digital currencies. Understanding the evolution of currency is important in understanding the current financial landscape and the potential for new forms of currency in the future.

Early Forms of Currency

The earliest forms of currency were based on the exchange of goods and services through bartering. Individuals would exchange goods or services of equal value, with no physical currency involved. This system was difficult to manage and not scalable, leading to the development of alternative forms of currency.

Commodity Money

Commodity money emerged as a solution to the limitations of bartering. Commodity money is any item that has intrinsic value and can be used as a medium of exchange. Common examples include precious metals like gold and silver, as well as salt and other valuable resources. Commodity money was often used in the form of coins, which were minted by governments and had a standardized weight and purity.

Fiat Currency

Fiat currency is a currency that has no intrinsic value and is only valuable because of the government's authority and the trust of the people using it. Fiat currencies are not backed by any physical commodity or precious metal, but rather by the faith of the people using the currency. The first fiat currency was introduced in China during the Tang Dynasty in the 7th century.

Paper Money

Paper money emerged as a more practical and convenient form of currency than physical coins. The first paper currency was introduced in China during the 7th century, and was later adopted by European countries in the 17th century. Paper money is essentially a promissory note that represents a certain amount of gold or other physical currency. This allowed governments to print more money than they had in physical reserves, increasing the money supply and allowing for greater economic growth.

Digital Currency

Digital currency is the most recent evolution in the history of currency. Digital currencies are decentralized and often use blockchain technology to create a secure and transparent ledger of all transactions. Bitcoin, the first and most well-known digital currency, was introduced in 2009 by an anonymous individual or group using the pseudonym Satoshi Nakamoto. Since then, numerous other digital currencies have emerged, each with their own unique features and uses.

The Future of Currency

As technology continues to advance, it is likely that the concept of currency will continue to evolve. Digital currencies are already being adopted by a growing number of businesses and individuals, and may eventually become the dominant form of currency. Additionally, the rise of decentralized finance (DeFi) and blockchain technology has the potential to disrupt traditional financial institutions and change the way we think about money and financial transactions.

In conclusion, the evolution of currency has been a long and complex process, with numerous forms of currency emerging and evolving over time. From bartering and commodity money to fiat currency and digital currency, each form of currency has had its own unique advantages and disadvantages. As technology continues to advance, it is likely that new forms of currency will continue to emerge, changing the way we think about money and financial transactions.

The Role of Money in Society

Money plays a significant role in modern society, and its impact extends beyond simple transactions. It is a unit of account, a store of value, and a medium of exchange. The role of money in society can be analyzed from different angles, including economic, social, and cultural perspectives. In this chapter, we will explore the various roles that money plays in society.

Economic Role of Money

From an economic perspective, money serves as a tool for exchanging goods and services. Money enables people to exchange goods and services without the need for barter, which can be difficult and time-consuming. For example, if someone wants to buy bread but only has oranges, they would need to find a baker who is willing to accept oranges as payment. Money makes this process much simpler and efficient, as the buyer can use cash, credit cards, or digital payments to complete the transaction.

Money also serves as a unit of account, providing a common measure for the value of goods and services. This means that people can compare the prices of different goods and services using a standardized unit of measurement. For example, a person can compare the price of bread to the price of milk, even though they are two different products.

Additionally, money functions as a store of value, allowing people to save their wealth and use it at a later time. This makes it possible to invest, plan for the future, and manage financial risk. Money can be used to purchase assets, such as real estate or stocks, which can appreciate in value over time, allowing individuals to build wealth.

Social Role of Money

The social role of money is also significant. It can be used to measure social status and to express power, prestige, and success. For example, people often use luxury goods, such as expensive cars or jewelry, to signal their wealth and social status. Similarly, high-income jobs, such as lawyers or doctors, are often viewed as prestigious and carry a certain level of social status.

Moreover, money can facilitate social relationships, such as gift-giving, charity, and social support. For example, people may give money to friends or family members as a gift or to support them in times of need. Money can also be used to support charitable organizations and social causes.

Cultural Role of Money

The cultural role of money is closely tied to its social and economic roles. Money has been the subject of art, literature, and cultural expression for centuries, reflecting the values and beliefs of society. Money has also been used to support cultural and artistic endeavors, such as funding the construction of buildings, museums, and theaters.

The cultural role of money also relates to its use in religious and spiritual practices. For example, money is used in many religions as an offering or a tithe. Some religions have specific guidelines on the use and handling of money, and money plays a significant role in religious practices, rituals, and ceremonies.

The Future of Money

The role of money in society is continually evolving, and the future of money is likely to be shaped by technology, changing social norms, and economic shifts. Digital currencies, such as Bitcoin and other cryptocurrencies, are changing the way people think about money and its role in society. These currencies are decentralized, meaning they are not controlled by governments or financial institutions. They allow for fast, secure, and low-cost transactions, making them a popular choice for online purchases and cross-border transactions.

In addition, the rise of mobile payments, such as Apple Pay and Google Wallet, is changing the way people use and interact with money. Mobile payments allow people to pay for goods and services with a simple tap or swipe, eliminating the need for cash or credit cards.

The future of money is likely to be shaped by a range of economic, social, and technological factors. As new forms of currency and payment emerge, the way we interact with money and conduct transactions is rapidly evolving. In this chapter, we will explore some of the potential future developments in the world of money and finance.

One of the most significant changes in the future of money is the continued rise of digital currencies, such as Bitcoin, Ethereum, and other cryptocurrencies. These currencies operate independently of traditional banking systems and rely on decentralized networks to verify transactions. This makes them highly secure and resistant to fraud or counterfeiting, as each transaction is recorded on a public ledger known as the blockchain.

As the popularity of digital currencies grows, they are increasingly being accepted by merchants and consumers as a valid form of payment. In fact, many online retailers and service providers already accept Bitcoin and other cryptocurrencies as a means of payment. This trend is likely to continue, as more and more people become comfortable with using digital currencies for day-to-day transactions.

Another potential development in the future of money is the rise of peer-to-peer lending and crowdfunding platforms. These platforms allow individuals to lend or invest money directly in other individuals or small businesses, cutting out traditional banking institutions and intermediaries. This can provide more efficient and cost-effective access to capital for individuals and small businesses, while also providing investors with higher returns on their investments.

Another potential trend in the future of money is the continued growth of fintech, or financial technology. Fintech startups are developing innovative new technologies to help people save, invest, and manage their money more effectively. These technologies include robo-advisors, which use algorithms and artificial intelligence to provide personalized investment advice, as well as mobile banking apps, which allow people to manage their finances from their smartphones.

As these and other technological developments continue to reshape the financial landscape, it is likely that the role of traditional banking institutions will continue to evolve. Some experts predict that traditional banks may eventually become obsolete, replaced by a more decentralized and peer-to-peer financial system.

In addition to these technological developments, the future of money is also likely to be shaped by broader economic and social trends. For example, the increasing globalization of trade and commerce is likely to lead to a more interconnected global financial system, where money can move seamlessly across borders and between currencies.

Furthermore, the growing awareness of social and environmental issues is also likely to influence the future of money. Many consumers are now looking for ways to invest their money in socially responsible companies and causes, while also minimizing their impact on the environment. This has led to the growth of impact investing, which focuses on generating positive social and environmental outcomes, as well as financial returns.

In conclusion, the future of money is likely to be shaped by a range of technological, economic, and social factors. As new forms of currency and payment continue to emerge, it is important for investors and consumers to stay informed and adapt to these changing trends. Whether through digital currencies, peer-to-peer lending platforms, or fintech innovations, the future of money promises to be both exciting and challenging.

The Future of Money

The future of money is a topic of much discussion and debate, as technological advancements and changing economic landscapes continue to reshape the way we interact with currency. From digital currencies and mobile payments to blockchain technology and decentralized finance, the possibilities for the future of money are endless.

One major trend in the future of money is the rise of digital currencies. Digital currencies are digital assets that can be used as a medium of exchange, store of value, or unit of account. They are often decentralized, meaning they are not controlled by a single entity or government. The most well-known digital currency is Bitcoin, which was introduced in 2009 and has since become a global phenomenon.

While Bitcoin and other digital currencies have had their fair share of controversies and setbacks, they have also demonstrated the potential for a new era of financial transactions that are faster, more secure, and more transparent than traditional currency transactions. In addition, digital currencies have the potential to provide financial services to millions of people who do not have access to traditional banking services, such as those in developing countries.

Another trend in the future of money is the rise of mobile payments. Mobile payments allow people to use their smartphones to make purchases and transfer money, without the need for cash or credit cards. This technology has already gained significant traction in countries like China, where mobile payment systems like Alipay and

WeChat Pay have become the primary payment method for many people.

The rise of mobile payments is expected to continue, as more and more people use smartphones as their primary device for accessing the internet and conducting financial transactions. In addition, advancements in biometric authentication technology, such as facial recognition and fingerprint scanning, are making mobile payments more secure and easier to use than ever before.

Another potential game-changer in the future of money is blockchain technology. Blockchain is a decentralized ledger technology that allows for secure, transparent, and tamper-proof transactions. It has already been used to create digital currencies like Bitcoin, but its potential goes far beyond that.

One potential use for blockchain technology is in the realm of smart contracts. Smart contracts are self-executing contracts with the terms of the agreement between buyer and seller being directly written into lines of code. This allows for more efficient and secure transactions, as well as the potential for new business models that are currently not possible with traditional contracts.

Decentralized finance (DeFi) is another potential game-changer in the future of money. DeFi refers to a set of financial services that are built on blockchain technology and do not rely on traditional financial institutions like banks or stock exchanges. Instead, they are built on decentralized networks, where users can interact with each other directly, without the need for intermediaries.

Some examples of DeFi services include decentralized exchanges, which allow users to trade digital assets without the need for a centralized exchange, and decentralized lending platforms, which allow users to lend and borrow money without the need for a traditional bank. These services are often more accessible, transparent, and cost-effective than their traditional counterparts, and they have the potential to disrupt the traditional financial system.

In addition to these technological advancements, the future of money will also be shaped by changing economic landscapes and social trends. For example, the rise of the gig economy and the increasing prevalence of remote work are changing the way people earn and spend money. As more people work as independent contractors or freelancers, they may require different financial services than traditional employees.

Similarly, the growing focus on sustainability and environmentalism is likely to impact the way people think about money. As consumers become more conscious of the environmental impact of their purchases, they may seek out financial services and investments that align with their values.

In conclusion, the future of money is likely to be shaped by a range of economic, social, and technological factors. While the specific developments that will shape the future of money are difficult to predict, it is clear that the trend towards digitization and decentralization is likely to continue, with blockchain and cryptocurrency at the forefront of these developments.

As technology continues to evolve and society becomes more comfortable with digital currencies, it is possible that traditional forms of currency, such as physical cash, may become less relevant. This shift towards digital currency could have significant implications for governments and financial institutions, as they may need to adapt their policies and systems to keep up with these changes.

Moreover, the rise of decentralized finance (DeFi) and blockchain-based financial systems could lead to more inclusive financial services, as people in underserved communities around the world gain access to banking and financial services for the first time. The use of blockchain technology could also enable greater transparency and accountability in the financial sector, reducing the risk of fraud and corruption.

However, the adoption of new forms of currency and payment systems will likely bring its own set of challenges, including regulatory issues and the potential for increased cybercrime. In addition, the development of new financial technologies may exacerbate existing social and economic inequalities if not managed properly.

In conclusion, the future of money is uncertain, but it is clear that new technologies will continue to shape the way we think about and use currency. As the world becomes more digitized and interconnected, it is likely that blockchain and cryptocurrency will play an increasingly important role in the global economy, providing new opportunities for innovation and growth, while also posing new risks and challenges that will need to be addressed.

In conclusion, cryptocurrency has emerged as a new form of money that has the potential to transform the way we think about currency and transactions. The rise of Bitcoin and other cryptocurrencies has challenged the traditional financial system and provided a new level of flexibility and security for investors and consumers alike.

However, the world of cryptocurrency is still new and rapidly evolving, and there are many risks and uncertainties associated with investing in these digital assets. It is important for investors to conduct their own research and understand the risks and rewards associated with investing in cryptocurrency.

Ultimately, the future of cryptocurrency is difficult to predict, but it is clear that this technology has the potential to disrupt and transform the traditional financial system in ways that we cannot yet imagine. As we continue to witness the evolution of money, it will be exciting to see how cryptocurrency and other innovations shape the financial landscape in the years to come.

CHAPTER 10 - CRYPTOCURRENCY

What is Cryptocurrency?
A Brief History of Cryptocurrency
Different Types of Cryptocurrency
Advantages and Disadvantages of Cryptocurrency
Cryptocurrency and its Impact on Society

What is Cryptocurrency?

Cryptocurrency is a digital or virtual currency that uses cryptography for security and operates independently of a central bank. It is a decentralized form of currency that allows for secure and anonymous transactions between individuals without the need for intermediaries like banks or other financial institutions.

At the core of cryptocurrency is a technology known as blockchain. A blockchain is a decentralized digital ledger that records transactions on multiple computers in a secure and transparent way. Each transaction is verified and recorded on the blockchain, creating a permanent and immutable record that cannot be altered or tampered with.

Cryptocurrencies are designed to be secure and transparent, with many offering high levels of anonymity to users. Transactions are conducted using digital wallets, which are secured by private keys that only the owner has access to. This means that users can conduct transactions with each other without the need for banks or other intermediaries.

The first and most well-known cryptocurrency is Bitcoin, which was created in 2009 by an anonymous individual or group using the pseudonym Satoshi Nakamoto. Bitcoin uses a decentralized network of computers to verify and record transactions, and has gained a reputation as a secure and reliable form of currency.

Other cryptocurrencies have since emerged, each with their own unique features and characteristics. Some, like Ethereum, are designed to facilitate the creation of decentralized applications, while others, like Litecoin, are designed to be faster and more efficient than Bitcoin.

Cryptocurrencies can be traded on digital exchanges, where users can buy and sell them for other forms of currency, such as US dollars or Euros. The value of cryptocurrencies can be highly volatile, with prices sometimes fluctuating dramatically in short periods of time.

One of the key advantages of cryptocurrencies is their ability to operate independently of traditional financial institutions. This means that users can conduct transactions with each other without the need for banks or other intermediaries, which can be faster, more secure, and more cost-effective than traditional financial transactions.

However, there are also a number of risks and challenges associated with cryptocurrencies. One of the main concerns is their lack of regulation, which can make them vulnerable to fraud, hacking, and other forms of criminal activity. In addition, the highly volatile nature of cryptocurrency prices can make them a risky investment, and many experts advise caution when investing in cryptocurrencies.

Despite these challenges, the popularity of cryptocurrencies continues to grow, with more and more individuals and businesses adopting them as a form of payment. As the technology continues to develop, it is likely that we will see new and innovative uses for cryptocurrencies, and they may play an increasingly important role in the global economy in the years to come.

A Brief History of Cryptocurrency

Cryptocurrency has become a buzzword in recent years, but the concept of digital currency is not new. In fact, the history of cryptocurrency can be traced back several decades. In this chapter, we will explore the brief history of cryptocurrency, including its roots in digital currencies and the development of blockchain technology.

The origins of digital currencies can be traced back to the 1980s and 1990s, when companies like DigiCash and eCash attempted to create a digital payment system that would allow for secure, anonymous transactions. These early efforts were hampered by a lack of widespread adoption and concerns about security and fraud.

It wasn't until 2009 that the first successful cryptocurrency, Bitcoin, was introduced to the world. Bitcoin was created by an anonymous individual or group of individuals using the pseudonym Satoshi Nakamoto. The original Bitcoin whitepaper, published in October 2008, outlined a new electronic cash system that would operate independently of a central authority.

The concept of a decentralized, peer-to-peer payment system was revolutionary, and Bitcoin quickly gained a following among early adopters and tech enthusiasts. Bitcoin transactions were recorded on a public ledger called the blockchain, which was maintained by a network of computers around the world.

Bitcoin's early success inspired the creation of other cryptocurrencies, including Litecoin, Ripple, and Ethereum. Each of these cryptocurrencies had its own unique features and capabilities, but all shared the core principles of decentralization, security, and transparency.

In the years since Bitcoin's creation, the cryptocurrency market has experienced significant growth and volatility. At its peak in late 2017, the total market capitalization of all cryptocurrencies reached nearly $830 billion, before crashing to around $130 billion a year later.

Despite its ups and downs, cryptocurrency has continued to attract the attention of investors, entrepreneurs, and tech enthusiasts around the world. The potential benefits of decentralized digital currencies, such as greater financial freedom and increased transparency, continue to drive innovation and development in the space.

As the cryptocurrency market continues to evolve, new technologies and applications are emerging that could further transform the way we think about money and finance. One of the most exciting developments in recent years has been the rise of decentralized finance, or DeFi, which aims to create a more open and accessible financial system using blockchain technology.

Overall, the brief history of cryptocurrency has been characterized by innovation, experimentation, and disruption. While it is still too early to predict the future of cryptocurrency with certainty, it is clear that digital currencies have the potential to fundamentally change the way we think about money and finance.

Different Types of Cryptocurrency

Cryptocurrency has come a long way since Bitcoin, which was the first decentralized digital currency, was introduced in 2009. Today, there are thousands of different cryptocurrencies available, each with unique features and use cases. In this chapter, we will explore the different types of cryptocurrency and what sets them apart.

Bitcoin

Bitcoin was the first cryptocurrency and remains the most well-known and widely used. It operates on a decentralized network, meaning that there is no central authority controlling the currency. Instead, transactions are validated by a network of computers, and the records are stored on a public ledger called the blockchain. Bitcoin is limited to a maximum supply of 21 million coins, and it is widely used for online purchases, international money transfers, and as a store of value.

Ethereum

Ethereum is a decentralized platform that enables the creation of smart contracts and decentralized applications (DApps). It was launched in 2015 and is the second-largest cryptocurrency by market capitalization. Ethereum operates on a blockchain, similar to Bitcoin, but it also allows developers to create and execute smart contracts. Smart contracts are self-executing contracts that are programmed to automatically execute when certain conditions are met. Ethereum is used for a variety of purposes, including the creation of DApps, fundraising through initial coin offerings (ICOs), and as a means of payment.

Ripple

Ripple is a payment protocol and cryptocurrency that was created in 2012. It is designed to facilitate fast and low-cost international money transfers. Ripple operates on a decentralized network, and it uses a consensus algorithm to validate transactions. Unlike Bitcoin and Ethereum, Ripple is not mined. Instead, all the Ripple tokens were created at once, and a portion of them are released to the market each month. Ripple is used by financial institutions and payment providers to facilitate cross-border payments.

Litecoin

Litecoin was created in 2011 as a fork of Bitcoin. It operates on a decentralized network, similar to Bitcoin, but with a few key differences. Litecoin has a faster block generation time and uses a different hashing algorithm, which makes it more efficient for mining with consumer-grade hardware. Litecoin is often used for online purchases and as a store of value.

Bitcoin Cash
Bitcoin Cash was created in 2017 as a fork of Bitcoin. It was created to address some of the scaling issues that Bitcoin was facing, specifically the slow transaction times and high fees. Bitcoin Cash operates on a decentralized network, similar to Bitcoin, but with a larger block size limit, which allows for faster and cheaper transactions. Bitcoin Cash is often used for online purchases and as a means of payment.

Cardano

Cardano is a decentralized platform that was launched in 2017. It is designed to enable the creation of smart contracts and DApps, similar to Ethereum. However, Cardano uses a proof-of-stake consensus algorithm, which is more energy-efficient than the proof-of-work algorithm used by Bitcoin and Ethereum. Cardano is often used for the creation of DApps, fundraising through ICOs, and as a store of value.

Polkadot

Polkadot is a decentralized platform that was launched in 2020. It is designed to enable the creation of interoperable blockchains, meaning that different blockchains can communicate and work together seamlessly. Polkadot uses a proof-of-stake consensus algorithm and is often used for the creation of DApps, fundraising through ICOs, and as a store of value.

Binance Coin

Binance Coin is a cryptocurrency that was created by Binance, one of the largest cryptocurrency exchanges in the world. It operates on a decentralized network, and it is used as a means of payment on the Binance exchange. Binance Coin is often used for trading fees, listing fees,and other transactional fees within the Binance ecosystem. As the Binance exchange has grown in popularity, the value of Binance Coin has also increased. As of September 2021, Binance Coin had a market cap of over $50 billion, making it one of the largest cryptocurrencies in the world.

Ripple (XRP)

Ripple is a cryptocurrency that was designed for global payments and is often used by banks and financial institutions. The Ripple network uses a unique consensus algorithm called the Ripple Protocol Consensus Algorithm (RPCA), which allows for fast and secure transactions. Unlike other cryptocurrencies, Ripple is centralized and is controlled by the company Ripple Labs. Ripple has been controversial due to its centralized nature, and it has faced legal challenges over whether it qualifies as a security.

Polkadot (DOT)

Polkadot is a newer cryptocurrency that was created in 2020. It is a multi-chain network that allows different blockchain networks to communicate and interact with each other. Polkadot aims to solve the problem of interoperability between different blockchains, making it easier for developers to create decentralized applications that can communicate with each other. The value of Polkadot has grown significantly since its creation, and it is now one of the top 10 cryptocurrencies by market capitalization.

Dogecoin (DOGE)

Dogecoin is a cryptocurrency that was created in 2013 as a joke. It features the popular "Doge" internet meme as its logo and has gained a cult following among cryptocurrency enthusiasts. Despite its origins as a joke, Dogecoin has gained significant value in recent years, thanks in part to support from celebrities like Elon Musk. Dogecoin has faced criticism due to its lack of development and its reliance on memes for marketing.

Cardano (ADA)

Cardano is a cryptocurrency that was created in 2017 and was designed to be a more sustainable and secure alternative to other cryptocurrencies. Cardano uses a unique proof-of-stake consensus algorithm called Ouroboros, which is designed to be more energy-efficient than the proof-of-work algorithm used by Bitcoin. Cardano has gained popularity due to its focus on sustainability and its ability to support decentralized applications.

Ethereum Classic (ETC)

Ethereum Classic is a cryptocurrency that was created in 2016 as a fork of the Ethereum blockchain. It was created after the Ethereum community split over a contentious proposal to reverse a hack that had occurred on the Ethereum blockchain. Ethereum Classic is designed to be a more decentralized and immutable version of Ethereum, with no central authority controlling the network.

Conclusion

Cryptocurrency is a rapidly evolving and complex field, with new cryptocurrencies and use cases emerging all the time. Understanding the different types of cryptocurrency and their unique features is essential for anyone looking to invest in or use cryptocurrency. While Bitcoin remains the dominant cryptocurrency, other cryptocurrencies like Ethereum, Binance Coin, and Polkadot are growing in popularity and value. As the field of cryptocurrency continues to evolve, it is important to stay informed and up to date on the latest developments and trends.

Advantages and Disadvantages of Cryptocurrency

Cryptocurrency has gained significant popularity in recent years as a new form of digital currency. While many individuals and businesses have embraced the use of cryptocurrency, others remain skeptical due to the various advantages and disadvantages associated with this currency. In this chapter, we will explore the advantages and disadvantages of cryptocurrency.

Advantages of Cryptocurrency

Decentralized: One of the primary advantages of cryptocurrency is that it is decentralized. Unlike traditional currency, which is controlled by banks and other financial institutions, cryptocurrency is decentralized, meaning that it is not controlled by any central authority. This makes it more secure, as there is no central point of failure that can be targeted by hackers.

Anonymity: Another advantage of cryptocurrency is that it is often anonymous. While this anonymity can raise concerns about illegal activities such as money laundering, it can also be beneficial for individuals who want to maintain their privacy.

Security: Cryptocurrency is more secure than traditional currency due to its use of blockchain technology. Transactions on a blockchain are secured through a complex mathematical algorithm, making them nearly impossible to hack or manipulate.

Accessibility: Cryptocurrency is accessible to anyone with an internet connection, regardless of their location. This makes it an ideal option for individuals who do not have access to traditional banking services.

Low Transaction Fees: Unlike traditional banking transactions that can have high transaction fees, cryptocurrency transactions often have low or no transaction fees.

Disadvantages of Cryptocurrency

Volatility: One of the main disadvantages of cryptocurrency is its high volatility. The value of cryptocurrencies can fluctuate rapidly, which can make it a risky investment. While some individuals have made significant profits from investing in cryptocurrencies, others have lost a significant amount of money due to their volatility.

Acceptance: Another disadvantage of cryptocurrency is that it is not widely accepted. While there are some merchants and businesses that accept cryptocurrency, many do not, which can make it difficult for individuals to use cryptocurrency as a form of payment.

Complexity: Cryptocurrency is a complex technology, and it can be difficult for individuals who are not tech-savvy to understand. The process of buying, selling, and storing cryptocurrency can be complicated, which can be a barrier for some individuals.

Regulation: The lack of regulation surrounding cryptocurrency can be a disadvantage. While some individuals appreciate the lack of government intervention, others are concerned that the lack of regulation makes cryptocurrency more vulnerable to fraud and other illegal activities.

Security Concerns: While cryptocurrency is generally considered more secure than traditional currency, there are still security concerns. Cryptocurrency exchanges have been targeted by hackers in the past, resulting in the theft of millions of dollars worth of cryptocurrency.

Conclusion

In conclusion, while there are advantages and disadvantages associated with cryptocurrency, it is clear that this new form of digital currency has significant potential to change the way we think about money. The decentralization, security, and accessibility of cryptocurrency make it an attractive option for many individuals and businesses, while the volatility and complexity of cryptocurrency remain concerns for others. As cryptocurrency continues to evolve and become more widely accepted, it is likely that its advantages will outweigh its disadvantages, making it an increasingly popular option for individuals and businesses alike.

Cryptocurrency and its Impact on Society

Cryptocurrency has been a topic of discussion for several years now, and it is rapidly gaining traction in the mainstream as an alternative to traditional forms of currency. The technology that powers cryptocurrency, blockchain, has also garnered significant attention as a potential disruptor to various industries. In this chapter, we will explore the impact of cryptocurrency on society, including its potential benefits and drawbacks.

Decentralization and Empowerment

One of the most significant potential benefits of cryptocurrency is its decentralized nature. Unlike traditional currency, which is controlled by governments and financial institutions, cryptocurrency operates on a decentralized network, which means it is not controlled by a single entity. This decentralization has the potential to empower individuals and communities, particularly those in countries with unstable political and economic systems.

Cryptocurrency allows individuals to transact with each other directly, without the need for intermediaries such as banks or government agencies. This means that people can send and receive money without having to go through a central authority, which can be particularly important in countries with corrupt governments or unstable financial systems.

Moreover, cryptocurrency can be used as a means of financial inclusion, allowing people who are unbanked or underbanked to participate in the global economy. Cryptocurrency can also provide an alternative to traditional financial systems for people who are distrustful of banks or for those who have been denied access to traditional banking services.

Transparency and Security

Another potential benefit of cryptocurrency is the level of transparency and security it provides. Transactions made on a blockchain are transparent and cannot be altered or deleted, making them highly secure. Blockchain technology provides a distributed ledger system that is almost impossible to hack or corrupt. Additionally, transactions can be made anonymously, which can be an advantage for people who value their privacy.

The use of blockchain technology also has the potential to reduce fraud and corruption. The transparency and security of blockchain technology make it an ideal tool for preventing fraud and ensuring the integrity of financial transactions. By removing the need for intermediaries, such as banks, cryptocurrency can reduce the risk of fraud and corruption in financial transactions.

Globalization and Financial Integration

Cryptocurrency has the potential to be a major force for globalization and financial integration. Cryptocurrency transactions can be conducted across borders, without the need for currency conversions or intermediaries. This can lead to increased trade and economic integration, which can be a significant benefit for developing economies.

Moreover, cryptocurrency can provide an alternative to traditional financial systems for people living in countries with unstable currencies. Cryptocurrency provides a stable store of value, which can be particularly important in countries with hyperinflation or currency devaluation. Cryptocurrency can also help to mitigate the impact of capital controls, which can be imposed by governments to restrict the movement of money across borders.

Potential Drawbacks

While cryptocurrency has many potential benefits, there are also significant drawbacks to consider. One of the most significant challenges facing cryptocurrency is its lack of regulation. Cryptocurrency operates in a legal grey area, which has led to concerns about its use in criminal activities such as money laundering and terrorism financing.

Moreover, the lack of regulation makes it difficult for consumers to seek redress if they are defrauded or if their assets are lost or stolen. Cryptocurrency is also highly volatile, with prices fluctuating dramatically in short periods. This volatility makes it difficult to use cryptocurrency as a store of value, which is one of the key functions of traditional currency.

Another significant drawback of cryptocurrency is its reliance on technology. Blockchain technology is still in its early stages of development, and there are concerns about its scalability and security. There is also the risk of cyber-attacks, which can result in the loss of large sums of money.

Additionally, the anonymity of cryptocurrency transactions can be a double-edged sword. While it can be an advantage for people who value their privacy, it can also be used to facilitate criminal activities such as money laundering, terrorism financing, and tax evasion. Cryptocurrencies have also been associated with illegal activities such as the sale of drugs and weapons on dark web marketplaces.

The impact of cryptocurrency on society is still evolving, and there are both positive and negative consequences. One potential benefit of cryptocurrency is the ability to increase financial inclusion, particularly for people who do not have access to traditional banking services. Cryptocurrency can also provide a means of payment for people in countries with unstable currencies or limited access to financial systems.

Furthermore, cryptocurrency has the potential to provide a more secure and transparent way of conducting transactions. Blockchain technology, which underlies most cryptocurrencies, is a decentralized ledger that records transactions in a secure and transparent way. This makes it difficult for anyone to tamper with the transaction history or manipulate the system.

Another advantage of cryptocurrency is its potential to lower transaction costs. Traditional financial transactions often involve intermediaries, such as banks and payment processors, which can add significant fees to the transaction. With cryptocurrency, transactions can be conducted directly between parties, eliminating the need for intermediaries and reducing the associated fees.

However, the impact of cryptocurrency on society is not all positive. One concern is the potential for cryptocurrencies to contribute to economic instability. Because cryptocurrencies are not backed by any government or financial institution, their value can be highly volatile and subject to significant fluctuations. This volatility can lead to financial losses for investors and uncertainty in the broader economy.

Additionally, the lack of regulation in the cryptocurrency market can lead to fraud and scams. Cryptocurrency exchanges, where people buy and sell cryptocurrencies, are often unregulated, which can make them vulnerable to hacks and thefts. As a result, investors in cryptocurrency may face risks such as losing their investments or having their digital wallets hacked.

The impact of cryptocurrency on society is also influenced by its environmental impact. The process of mining cryptocurrency, which involves solving complex mathematical algorithms to validate transactions on the blockchain, requires significant amounts of energy. As the popularity of cryptocurrency grows, so does the demand for energy-intensive mining operations, which can have a negative impact on the environment.

In conclusion, the impact of cryptocurrency on society is complex and multifaceted. While it has the potential to increase financial inclusion, provide a more secure and transparent way of conducting transactions, and lower transaction costs, it also presents risks such as economic instability, fraud, and environmental impact. As the use of cryptocurrency continues to grow and evolve, it will be important to strike a balance between the potential benefits and risks in order to ensure a positive impact on society.

In conclusion, cryptocurrency is a revolutionary digital asset that has the potential to change the way we think about money and finance. With its decentralized nature, fast transaction speeds, and strong security features, it offers many advantages over traditional forms of currency. However, it also presents its own unique set of challenges, such as regulatory and legal concerns, volatility, and the potential for criminal activities.

As cryptocurrency continues to evolve, it is important for individuals, businesses, and governments to stay informed and educated about its potential benefits and risks. It is also important to consider how cryptocurrency can be integrated into existing financial systems to drive innovation and create new opportunities for growth.

Ultimately, the future of cryptocurrency remains to be seen, but one thing is clear: it has the potential to reshape the way we think about money and the global economy.

CHAPTER 11 - BLOCKCHAIN BASICS

- ❖ What is Blockchain?
- ❖ How Does Blockchain Work?
- ❖ Components of a Blockchain
- ❖ Types of Blockchain
- ❖ Security Concerns in Blockchain

What is Blockchain?

Blockchain technology is a revolutionary concept that has the potential to transform the way we store, manage, and transmit data. At its core, a blockchain is a digital ledger that records transactions in a secure, decentralized, and transparent manner. It was first introduced in 2008 as the underlying technology behind Bitcoin, the world's first decentralized digital currency. Since then, blockchain has grown to become an increasingly popular technology with a wide range of applications across various industries.

In simple terms, a blockchain is a digital ledger that records transactions between two parties in a secure and tamper-proof manner. Each block in the chain contains a record of multiple transactions, and each block is linked to the previous block in the chain, forming a "chain" of blocks. The information contained within each block is encrypted and stored in multiple locations, making it nearly impossible to alter or manipulate the data.

Blockchain technology has the potential to revolutionize a variety of industries by enabling secure, decentralized, and transparent record-keeping. It has already been applied in industries such as finance, healthcare, and logistics, with new use cases emerging all the time. In this chapter, we will explore the basics of blockchain technology, how it works, and its potential impact on various industries.

How Does Blockchain Work?

Blockchain is a distributed ledger technology that enables secure and transparent recording of data. The technology was originally developed to support cryptocurrencies such as Bitcoin, but its potential applications extend far beyond this use case. Blockchain has the potential to revolutionize the way information is stored and shared, by providing a decentralized and secure way of recording and verifying data.

At its core, a blockchain is a digital ledger that records transactions or other data. However, unlike traditional databases, blockchains are decentralized, which means they are not owned or controlled by a single entity. Instead, they are maintained by a network of users, who collectively validate and verify transactions and other data.

The basic components of a blockchain are blocks, which contain information about transactions or other data, and a chain, which links the blocks together in chronological order. Each block contains a unique digital signature, called a hash, which is generated using a cryptographic algorithm. This hash serves as a kind of digital fingerprint for the block, allowing it to be easily identified and verified.

To add a new block to the blockchain, it must be validated by the network of users, a process known as consensus. This process involves a complex mathematical algorithm that requires a significant amount of computational power to solve. This algorithm is designed to ensure that each block is valid and unique, and that no two blocks can be added to the blockchain at the same time.

Once a block has been validated and added to the blockchain, it is immutable, which means it cannot be altered or deleted. This is because each block contains a reference to the previous block in the chain, as well as the hash of the previous block. If someone were to try to change a block in the chain, it would require changing all of the subsequent blocks in the chain, which is practically impossible due to the computational resources required.

The decentralized and immutable nature of blockchain has a number of important benefits. For one, it makes the technology extremely secure, since there is no single point of failure or attack. Additionally, the transparency and auditability of the technology make it well-suited for use cases where trust and transparency are critical, such as in supply chain management or financial transactions.

There are several different types of blockchain, each with their own unique features and use cases. Some blockchains, like Bitcoin, are designed primarily for financial transactions, while others are designed for more general-purpose applications. Some blockchains, like Ethereum, support the development of smart contracts, which are self-executing contracts that can be used to automate a wide range of business processes.

In order to interact with a blockchain, users typically use a software application, known as a wallet. Wallets allow users to create and manage digital identities, known as addresses, which are used to send and receive digital assets, such as cryptocurrency. When a user sends a transaction, it is broadcast to the network, where it is validated and added to the blockchain.

Overall, the technology behind blockchain is complex and can be difficult to understand. However, its potential to revolutionize the way we store and share information is clear, and its applications are likely to expand rapidly in the coming years.

Components of a Blockchain

A blockchain is a distributed ledger technology that records transactions and stores data across a decentralized network. The technology uses a combination of cryptography and consensus mechanisms to ensure the integrity and security of the data. In order to understand how blockchain works, it is important to understand the components that make up this innovative technology.

Distributed Network

One of the most important components of a blockchain is the distributed network. Rather than being controlled by a central authority or server, a blockchain is a decentralized network of nodes or computers that work together to maintain the ledger. Each node on the network has a copy of the ledger, which is constantly updated as new transactions are added. This decentralized structure allows for greater security and transparency, as there is no single point of failure or control.

Blocks

The data on a blockchain is stored in blocks, which are added to the ledger in a chronological order. Each block contains a unique hash, which is a digital fingerprint that identifies the block and its contents. The hash also serves as a reference to the previous block in the chain, which creates a continuous, unbreakable chain of blocks. The blocks on a blockchain are linked together, forming the blockchain.

Transactions

A transaction is a record of a transfer of value or data from one party to another. On a blockchain, transactions are verified and processed by the network of nodes. Once a transaction is verified, it is added to a block and becomes part of the blockchain. Transactions on a blockchain are immutable, meaning they cannot be altered or deleted once they are added to the ledger.

Consensus Mechanism

In order to maintain the integrity and security of the data on a blockchain, a consensus mechanism is used to ensure that all nodes on the network agree on the validity of each transaction. There are several different consensus mechanisms used in blockchain technology, including proof of work (PoW), proof of stake (PoS), and delegated proof of stake (DPoS). These mechanisms require network nodes to compete or collaborate in order to validate transactions and add them to the blockchain.

Cryptography

Cryptography is an essential component of blockchain technology. It is used to secure transactions and protect the privacy of users. Each transaction on a blockchain is encrypted using a public key and a private key. The public key is shared with the network, while the private key is kept secret and known only to the owner of the transaction. This allows for secure and private transactions on the blockchain.

Smart Contracts

Smart contracts are self-executing contracts that are programmed to automatically execute when certain conditions are met. They are an essential component of blockchain technology, as they allow for the automation of complex transactions and the creation of decentralized applications (DApps). Smart contracts are coded in a programming language specific to the blockchain platform they are being built on, such as Solidity for Ethereum.

In conclusion, the components of a blockchain are what make this technology so innovative and disruptive. From the distributed network to the use of cryptography and smart contracts, each component plays a vital role in ensuring the security, transparency, and immutability of the data on the blockchain. As blockchain technology continues to evolve and gain acceptance, it is likely that new components and features will be added to further enhance the functionality and usefulness of this revolutionary technology.

Types of Blockchain

Blockchain technology has evolved over the years, and as a result, there are different types of blockchains that are currently in use. These types of blockchains differ in terms of their structure, their level of decentralization, their consensus mechanisms, and their intended uses.

In this chapter, we will explore the different types of blockchains and their unique features.

Public Blockchains

Public blockchains are the most well-known type of blockchain, and they are used by cryptocurrencies such as Bitcoin and Ethereum. These blockchains are completely decentralized, and anyone can join the network and participate in the validation of transactions. Transactions on public blockchains are publicly visible, and anyone can view them. Public blockchains operate on an open-source protocol, which allows anyone to access the code and contribute to the development of the blockchain.

Public blockchains use a consensus mechanism called Proof of Work (PoW) or Proof of Stake (PoS) to validate transactions. In PoW, miners compete to solve complex mathematical puzzles to validate transactions and create new blocks on the blockchain. In PoS, validators are chosen based on the number of tokens they hold and their willingness to participate in the validation process.

Private Blockchains

Private blockchains are used by organizations to facilitate secure and private transactions within a closed network. Private blockchains are not completely decentralized, as access to the blockchain is restricted to authorized parties. The use of private blockchains allows organizations to maintain control over their data and ensure that sensitive information is kept private.

Unlike public blockchains, private blockchains use a consensus mechanism that does not require significant computational power. This allows private blockchains to process transactions faster and at a lower cost than public blockchains. Private blockchains also have a higher degree of scalability, as the number of transactions they can process is not limited by the constraints of a public network.

Consortium Blockchains

Consortium blockchains are a hybrid of public and private blockchains. In a consortium blockchain, a group of organizations collaborates to form a blockchain network that is not accessible to the public. The participating organizations maintain control over the blockchain and the data that is stored on it.

Consortium blockchains offer a balance between the security and privacy of private blockchains and the decentralized nature of public blockchains. They are often used in industries such as finance and healthcare, where multiple organizations need to collaborate and share data while maintaining the security and privacy of sensitive information.

Hybrid Blockchains

Hybrid blockchains are a combination of public and private blockchains. In a hybrid blockchain, some parts of the blockchain are public, while others are private. This allows organizations to maintain control over their data while still benefiting from the decentralized nature of public blockchains.

Hybrid blockchains are often used in applications where privacy is important, but the network still needs to be accessible to the public. They are also useful in situations where a large number of transactions need to be processed quickly and efficiently.

Sidechains

Sidechains are separate blockchains that are attached to a main blockchain. Sidechains are used to address the scalability issues of main blockchains, which may not be able to handle a large volume of transactions. By creating a sidechain, transactions can be processed more quickly and at a lower cost than on the main blockchain.

Sidechains can be used for a wide range of applications, including the creation of new tokens and the execution of smart contracts. Sidechains can also be used to test new blockchain applications before they are implemented on the main blockchain.

Permissioned Blockchains

Permissioned blockchains are similar to private blockchains in that access to the network is restricted to authorized parties. However, permissioned blockchains are designed to beused in collaborative environments where multiple organizations or entities need to share data and collaborate on a common goal. These blockchains are also known as consortium blockchains.

In permissioned blockchains, access to the network is controlled by a central authority or a group of authorities, who can grant or revoke access to users based on predefined criteria. This approach provides a higher level of security than public blockchains, as only authorized participants can contribute to the network.

The consensus mechanism used in permissioned blockchains can vary, depending on the use case and the specific requirements of the network. Some permissioned blockchains use Proof of Authority (PoA), which relies on a pre-selected group of validators to verify transactions and create new blocks. Other permissioned blockchains use Proof of Stake (PoS), which uses a stake-based system to determine who can validate transactions.

Permissioned blockchains are being used in a wide range of applications, including supply chain management, healthcare, finance, and more. For example, the R3 consortium, which includes more than 200 financial institutions, has developed a permissioned blockchain called Corda that is designed to facilitate secure and efficient financial transactions.

Hybrid Blockchains

As the name suggests, hybrid blockchains combine elements of both public and private blockchains. Hybrid blockchains are designed to provide the benefits of both types of blockchains while mitigating some of their drawbacks.

In a hybrid blockchain, the public-facing layer is used for tasks such as identity verification, while the private layer is used for sensitive transactions. This approach provides a higher level of security than public blockchains while still allowing for a degree of transparency.

Hybrid blockchains can also be used to address the scalability issues that are commonly associated with public blockchains. By moving some of the data off the public-facing layer, hybrid blockchains can reduce the amount of data that needs to be stored and processed on the public blockchain.

One example of a hybrid blockchain is Dragonchain, which was developed by the Disney company. Dragonchain is a hybrid blockchain that allows organizations to build and run their own private blockchains while still benefiting from the security and transparency of a public blockchain.

Conclusion

Blockchain technology is a rapidly evolving field that is transforming many aspects of modern life. While blockchain was originally developed to support cryptocurrencies like Bitcoin, it has since grown to encompass a wide range of applications and use cases.

Blockchain is still in its early stages, and there is much that remains to be discovered and developed. As the technology continues to mature, we can expect to see even more innovative applications of blockchain in fields like healthcare, finance, supply chain management, and beyond.

By understanding the different types of blockchains, their components, and how they work, we can gain a deeper appreciation of this exciting and rapidly evolving technology. Whether you are a developer, investor, or simply an interested observer, blockchain is a technology that is well worth exploring in greater detail.

Security Concerns in Blockchain

Blockchain technology has been touted as an innovation that could change the world. However, like any new technology, it is not without its challenges and concerns. One of the biggest issues surrounding blockchain is security.

While blockchain is designed to be secure and transparent, it is still vulnerable to attacks and security breaches. In this chapter, we will examine the security concerns in blockchain and the measures that can be taken to address them.

The Vulnerability of Decentralized Systems

One of the key features of blockchain is that it is a decentralized system. This means that there is no central authority or control. Instead, the network is made up of a series of nodes, which work together to validate transactions and create new blocks. While this has many advantages, it also makes the system vulnerable to attack.

One of the most common attacks on blockchain is the 51% attack. In this scenario, a single entity controls more than 50% of the computing power in the network. With this level of control, the attacker can manipulate the blockchain, adding or removing transactions and even creating new coins. This type of attack is particularly dangerous in a proof-of-work system, where the attacker can use their computing power to generate fake transactions and double-spend coins.

Another type of attack is the Sybil attack, which involves creating multiple identities or nodes to manipulate the network. In a decentralized system, it is difficult to distinguish between legitimate and fake nodes, which makes it easier for an attacker to gain control of the network.

Smart Contract Vulnerabilities

Smart contracts are another area of concern when it comes to blockchain security. Smart contracts are self-executing contracts that are written in code and stored on the blockchain. They can be used for a wide range of applications, from financial transactions to supply chain management.

However, if the code in a smart contract is not properly written, it can lead to vulnerabilities and security breaches. One of the most infamous examples of this is the DAO hack, which occurred in 2016. The DAO was a decentralized autonomous organization that was built on the Ethereum blockchain. It was designed to allow members to vote on which projects to fund, and the funds were managed by a series of smart contracts.

However, a vulnerability in one of the smart contracts allowed an attacker to siphon off a large portion of the funds. This highlighted the need for better auditing and testing of smart contracts, as well as the importance of having a mechanism in place to deal with security breaches.

Privacy Concerns

While blockchain is designed to be transparent, this can be a double-edged sword when it comes to privacy. The public nature of the blockchain means that all transactions are visible to anyone with access to the network. While this is great for transparency and accountability, it also means that personal information and sensitive data can be exposed.

There are several approaches to addressing the privacy concerns of blockchain. One approach is to use a permissioned blockchain, where access to the network is restricted to authorized parties. Another approach is to use a privacy-focused blockchain, such as Monero or Zcash, which use techniques like zero-knowledge proofs and ring signatures to obfuscate transaction data.

Regulatory Compliance

Another area of concern when it comes to blockchain is regulatory compliance. While blockchain is designed to be decentralized and autonomous, this can make it difficult to comply with existing regulations and laws. For example, anti-money laundering (AML) and know-your-customer (KYC) regulations require financial institutions to collect and verify customer information.

This can be challenging in a decentralized system where there is no central authority to perform these functions. However, there are efforts underway to address this issue. For example, some blockchain projects are working on developing identity solutions that can be used to verify users without compromising their privacy.

Conclusion

Blockchain has the potential to transform industries and change the way we conduct transactions and exchange value. However, as with any emerging technology, it is not without its challenges and limitations.

One of the most significant concerns regarding blockchain is security. While blockchain technology itself is highly secure, there are still vulnerabilities and risks associated with using it. As discussed in this chapter, some of the major security concerns in blockchain include hacking, 51% attacks, and smart contract vulnerabilities.

To address these concerns, it is essential to prioritize security at every level of blockchain development, from the initial design and implementation to ongoing monitoring and maintenance. This includes using secure coding practices, performing regular security audits, and staying up-to-date with the latest security protocols and best practices.

Another important consideration when it comes to blockchain security is regulatory compliance. As blockchain continues to gain widespread adoption, governments and regulatory bodies around the world are taking a closer look at how to regulate and oversee blockchain-based transactions. This includes addressing issues related to anti-money laundering (AML) and know your customer (KYC) regulations, as well as ensuring that blockchain-based transactions comply with existing financial and securities laws.

In addition to security and regulatory concerns, there are also issues related to scalability and interoperability that need to be addressed. While blockchain has the potential to revolutionize a wide range of industries, the current limitations on transaction speed and volume can make it difficult to implement on a large scale. Furthermore, the lack of interoperability between different blockchain platforms can create barriers to adoption and hinder collaboration and innovation.

Despite these challenges, blockchain remains a highly promising technology that has the potential to transform a wide range of industries and change the way we interact with each other and exchange value. With ongoing research and development, as well as a commitment to addressing the various concerns and limitations of the technology, blockchain is poised to become an even more powerful tool for innovation and growth in the years to come.

Investing 101: A Beginner's Guide to Building Wealth

CHAPTER 12 - THE BUSINESS OF BLOCKCHAIN

Industries that Use Blockchain Technology
Adding Value to Your Business with Blockchain
Growing Money with Blockchain
The Cloud and Blockchain
Blockchain and Gaming
Supply Chain Management and Blockchain
Blockchain Technology and Quality Assurance

Industries that Use Blockchain Technology

Blockchain technology has revolutionized industries across the globe, thanks to its decentralized nature, immutable records, and secure architecture. It has disrupted numerous sectors, offering streamlined and efficient solutions for complex problems. In this chapter, we will explore various industries that use blockchain technology.

Financial Services

The financial services industry has been the early adopters of blockchain technology. The blockchain's immutable and secure ledger system eliminates the need for intermediaries, saving significant amounts of time and money. Cryptocurrencies, smart contracts, and distributed ledgers are changing the way banks and other financial institutions conduct transactions, including asset trading, cross-border payments, and money transfer.

Healthcare

Blockchain technology has enormous potential in the healthcare sector. The blockchain can help to secure patient records, ensure privacy, and reduce the possibility of data breaches. Additionally, blockchain can provide solutions to supply chain management in the pharmaceutical industry. Blockchain technology can help reduce the risks of counterfeit drugs by tracking the origin and movement of each drug throughout the supply chain. This technology can potentially save lives by ensuring the safety and quality of drugs.

Retail

Retailers have begun to adopt blockchain technology to offer their customers a more transparent and secure supply chain. Blockchain can provide a secure and transparent ledger to track product information and authenticity, which can help to combat counterfeit products, as well as prevent supply chain fraud. Blockchain-based supply chain management can ensure product safety and quality, reduce waste, and boost consumer trust.

Real Estate

Real estate is one of the most significant investments people make in their lifetime. The blockchain's transparency, security, and immutability provide a unique opportunity for secure and efficient transactions. The technology can facilitate transparent property records, eliminating the need for intermediaries, including lawyers and real estate agents. It can also reduce the possibility of fraud and disputes related to property ownership.

Energy

Blockchain technology can play a crucial role in the energy sector. Blockchain can enable peer-to-peer transactions between energy producers and consumers, providing a secure and transparent energy exchange. In addition, blockchain technology can ensure the safety and security of the energy supply chain, by enabling real-time monitoring and tracking of energy sources, such as solar panels, wind turbines, and power plants.

Supply Chain Management

Supply chain management is a complex process that requires coordination between multiple parties, including suppliers, manufacturers, and distributors. Blockchain technology can provide transparency, traceability, and efficiency throughout the supply chain. The technology can enable real-time tracking and monitoring of products, reducing the possibility of fraud, counterfeiting, and supply chain errors.

Government

Blockchain technology can transform government services, improving efficiency and transparency. Blockchain-based voting systems can ensure that votes are accurately recorded, reducing the possibility of fraud and ensuring that each vote is counted. Additionally, blockchain can help to secure government records and provide a more efficient and transparent way to manage and share information.

Education

Blockchain technology can transform education by providing secure and transparent verification of student credentials. Blockchain can enable students to share their academic records with potential employers securely, reducing the possibility of fraud and ensuring that credentials are authentic. Additionally, blockchain can provide a secure and transparent way to record and verify professional development, ensuring that employees have the necessary skills and knowledge to perform their jobs.

In conclusion, blockchain technology has a vast range of applications across various industries. Blockchain technology's decentralized, secure, and transparent nature offers solutions for some of the most pressing issues in industries, including financial services, healthcare, retail, real estate, energy, supply chain management, government, and education. As more businesses recognize the potential of blockchain technology, the number of applications is likely to grow, and we can expect further innovation and disruption across industries.

Adding Value to Your Business with Blockchain

Blockchain technology is becoming increasingly popular across industries as a way to streamline operations, enhance security, and increase transparency. By adding value to businesses, blockchain is transforming the way they operate and interact with customers and partners. In this chapter, we will explore how businesses can add value to their operations with blockchain technology.

Enhanced Security

One of the most significant benefits of blockchain technology is enhanced security. The decentralized and distributed nature of blockchain technology makes it nearly impossible to hack or breach. In addition, the cryptographic algorithms used to secure the blockchain make it virtually tamper-proof.

This enhanced security can be valuable to businesses in a variety of ways. For example, supply chain management can be streamlined and made more secure with blockchain. By using blockchain to track the flow of goods, companies can ensure that products are authentic and have not been tampered with. This is particularly important for industries like pharmaceuticals, where counterfeit products can be dangerous or even deadly.

Increased Transparency

Another significant benefit of blockchain technology is increased transparency. By using blockchain to track the flow of goods, services, and transactions, businesses can ensure that everything is happening as it should be. This can help prevent fraud and ensure that all parties involved in a transaction are operating in good faith.

Increased transparency can also help build trust with customers and partners. By using blockchain to track the provenance of goods, companies can demonstrate that they are operating in an ethical and sustainable way. This can be particularly important for companies that are looking to differentiate themselves in crowded markets.

Streamlined Operations

Blockchain technology can also help streamline operations by automating processes and reducing the need for intermediaries. By using smart contracts, for example, businesses can automatically execute contracts when certain conditions are met. This can save time and money by eliminating the need for lawyers, banks, and other intermediaries.

In addition, blockchain technology can help businesses to more easily track and manage their assets. For example, by using blockchain to track inventory, businesses can ensure that they always have the right amount of stock on hand. This can help prevent stockouts and reduce the need for costly rush orders.

New Business Models

Finally, blockchain technology can enable new business models that were previously impossible. For example, blockchain can be used to create decentralized marketplaces, where buyers and sellers can interact directly without the need for intermediaries. This can be particularly valuable for small businesses that may not have the resources to compete in traditional markets.

In addition, blockchain technology can enable new forms of financing, such as initial coin offerings (ICOs). By using blockchain to create digital tokens that represent ownership in a company or project, businesses can raise capital in a new and innovative way. This can be particularly valuable for startups that are looking to raise capital but may not have access to traditional sources of funding.

Case Studies

There are already many examples of businesses that are using blockchain technology to add value to their operations. For example, Walmart is using blockchain to track the provenance of food products, making it easier to identify the source of any contamination in the event of a foodborne illness outbreak. In addition, Provenance is using blockchain to track the provenance of fish, enabling consumers to make more informed choices about the sustainability and ethical practices of the fishing industry.

Another example is Maersk, the world's largest shipping company, which is using blockchain technology to track the flow of goods across the supply chain. By using blockchain, Maersk has been able to reduce the time it takes to clear customs from days to minutes, saving time and reducing costs.

Conclusion

In conclusion, blockchain technology has the potential to add significant value to businesses across industries. By enhancing security, increasing transparency, streamlining operations, enabling new business models, and providing real-world case studies, blockchain can transform the way organizations operate and interact with customers and partners.

However, before implementing blockchain, businesses should consider the specific use cases and potential benefits to determine whether it is a good fit for their operations. In addition, they should assess the technical requirements and the resources needed to develop and maintain a blockchain solution.

Moreover, it is important to note that the technology is still in its early stages, and there are ongoing efforts to improve its scalability, interoperability, and privacy features. As the technology continues to evolve and mature, new opportunities may emerge for businesses to leverage blockchain in innovative ways.

In summary, adding value to a business with blockchain requires a strategic approach that aligns with the organization's goals and values. By identifying the right use cases, implementing effective security measures, ensuring regulatory compliance, and collaborating with stakeholders, businesses can leverage blockchain to unlock new opportunities for growth and innovation. As the technology continues to advance, it is clear that blockchain will play an increasingly important role in shaping the future of business and society.

Growing Money with Blockchain

The emergence of blockchain technology has provided new opportunities for individuals and businesses to grow their money. The technology's decentralized and secure nature makes it an ideal platform for investments, asset management, and trading. In this chapter, we will explore the different ways blockchain is being used to grow money and the potential benefits and risks involved.

Investing in Cryptocurrencies

One of the most popular ways to grow money with blockchain is by investing in cryptocurrencies. Bitcoin, the first and most well-known cryptocurrency, has seen a massive increase in value since its inception. In 2010, one Bitcoin was worth less than a penny. By 2017, its value had skyrocketed to nearly $20,000.

Cryptocurrencies are digital currencies that use blockchain technology to enable secure and transparent transactions without the need for intermediaries like banks. The value of cryptocurrencies is determined by supply and demand, with the limited supply of certain cryptocurrencies, such as Bitcoin, contributing to their perceived value. Investors can buy and hold cryptocurrencies with the expectation that their value will increase over time.

However, investing in cryptocurrencies is not without its risks. Cryptocurrencies are highly volatile and can experience significant price fluctuations in a short amount of time. The lack of regulation and oversight in the cryptocurrency market also makes it vulnerable to scams and fraud. It is essential to do thorough research and understand the risks involved before investing in cryptocurrencies.

Investing in Blockchain Startups

Investing in blockchain startups is another way to grow money with blockchain. Blockchain startups are companies that use blockchain technology to provide new solutions for various industries, such as finance, supply chain management, and healthcare. By investing in blockchain startups, individuals and businesses can gain exposure to the potential growth of the technology while supporting innovation and entrepreneurship.

Investing in blockchain startups can be done through initial coin offerings (ICOs), where companies issue their own digital tokens or coins that can be traded on cryptocurrency exchanges. However, investing in ICOs can be highly risky, as many of these companies are early-stage startups with untested business models and products. Investors must carefully research each company and its offering before investing.

Using Blockchain for Asset Management

Blockchain technology can also be used for asset management, providing a secure and transparent way to manage and track assets such as stocks, bonds, and real estate. The use of blockchain for asset management can reduce fraud, increase transparency, and streamline processes.

One example of blockchain being used for asset management is the security token offering (STO). STOs are a new type of digital investment vehicle that use blockchain to represent ownership in assets, such as real estate or company shares. STOs can be traded on cryptocurrency exchanges and provide a more accessible and transparent way to invest in traditional assets.

Using Blockchain for Trading

Blockchain technology is also being used to improve trading, providing more secure and transparent transactions. Decentralized exchanges (DEXs) use blockchain to enable peer-to-peer trading without the need for intermediaries like banks. This can reduce transaction fees, increase transaction speed, and provide greater privacy and security.

Centralized exchanges (CEXs) are traditional exchanges that use blockchain to provide additional security and transparency. By using blockchain to record and verify transactions, CEXs can reduce fraud, increase transparency, and provide greater security for traders.

Conclusion

In conclusion, blockchain technology provides new opportunities for individuals and businesses to grow their money through various investment vehicles, asset management solutions, and trading platforms. However, investing in blockchain and cryptocurrencies comes with risks and uncertainties, and it is essential to do thorough research and understand the technology and markets before investing. By utilizing blockchain technology for asset management and trading, individuals and businesses can benefit from greater security, transparency, and efficiency in financial transactions.

The Cloud and Blockchain

The cloud and blockchain are two of the most disruptive technologies of the 21st century. The cloud has revolutionized the way companies store and access their data, while blockchain has the potential to transform how we conduct transactions and store information. Together, the cloud and blockchain can create a powerful combination that can unlock new possibilities for businesses and organizations. In this chapter, we will explore the intersection of the cloud and blockchain, and how the two technologies can work together to deliver innovative solutions.

What is the Cloud?

Before we dive into the intersection of the cloud and blockchain, let's first define what the cloud is. The cloud refers to a network of remote servers that are used to store, manage, and process data. Instead of storing data on a local server or computer, companies can use the cloud to access and store data through the internet.

The cloud offers several advantages over traditional data storage methods. First, it is highly scalable, which means that companies can easily add or remove storage capacity as their needs change. Second, the cloud is cost-effective, as it eliminates the need for companies to purchase and maintain their own hardware. Finally, the cloud offers greater flexibility, as employees can access data from any location and any device, as long as they have an internet connection.

What is Blockchain?

Blockchain is a distributed ledger technology that is used to record and store data in a secure and transparent manner. The technology was initially created to enable the use of cryptocurrencies such as Bitcoin, but it has since been applied to a wide range of other use cases, such as supply chain management, voting systems, and more.

At its core, a blockchain is a digital ledger that is stored on a network of computers. Each block in the ledger contains a record of transactions, and each block is connected to the previous block, creating a chain of blocks. The data in the blockchain is immutable, meaning that once it is recorded, it cannot be altered or deleted. This makes the technology highly secure and transparent.

The Intersection of the Cloud and Blockchain

The cloud and blockchain are two distinct technologies, but they share several characteristics that make them complementary. Both technologies are distributed, meaning that data is stored across a network of computers rather than in a centralized location. This makes them more secure and resistant to cyber attacks. Additionally, both technologies are highly scalable, which means that they can be easily expanded as needed.

One of the key benefits of combining the cloud and blockchain is that it can increase the speed and efficiency of transactions. Since the cloud offers high-speed connectivity, it can be used to facilitate the exchange of data between blockchain nodes. This can enable faster and more efficient transactions, which can be particularly valuable in industries that require real-time data processing, such as finance or healthcare.

Another advantage of using the cloud and blockchain together is that it can make the technology more accessible to businesses of all sizes. By leveraging cloud infrastructure, businesses can reduce the costs and complexities of setting up their own blockchain networks. This can make it easier for smaller businesses to take advantage of the benefits of blockchain, such as increased security, transparency, and efficiency.

Use Cases for the Cloud and Blockchain

The cloud and blockchain can be used together in a wide range of use cases, from supply chain management to digital identity. Below are a few examples of how the two technologies can be combined to deliver innovative solutions:

Supply Chain Management

Supply chain management is one of the most promising use cases for the cloud and blockchain. By leveraging the cloud, businesses can create a shared, real-time view of the entire supply chain, from raw materials to finished products. This can enable greater transparency and accountability, as businesses can track the movement of goods and materials at every stage of the supply chain.

By using blockchain, businesses can create an immutable record of each transaction in the supply chain. This record can provide transparency and security, as no party can modify or delete the data. This can help to prevent fraud, counterfeit products, and other supply chain issues.

Blockchain can also help to optimize supply chain management by enabling smart contracts. Smart contracts are self-executing contracts with the terms of the agreement between buyer and seller being directly written into lines of code. They can automate processes such as payment and delivery, and can help to reduce costs, errors, and delays.

One example of a company using blockchain for supply chain management is IBM, which has developed a blockchain-based platform called IBM Food Trust. The platform enables food companies to track the movement of food products through the supply chain, from farm to table. This can help to reduce the risk of foodborne illnesses and can provide greater transparency for consumers.

Another example is Walmart, which has implemented blockchain technology to track the movement of pork in China. By using blockchain, Walmart is able to track the movement of pork from the farm to the store, providing greater transparency and accountability for consumers.

Overall, the cloud and blockchain can provide significant benefits for supply chain management, including increased transparency, accountability, and efficiency. As more businesses adopt these technologies, we can expect to see greater innovation and disruption in the supply chain industry.

Healthcare

The healthcare industry is another area that can benefit from the cloud and blockchain. By leveraging the cloud, healthcare providers can store and share patient data more securely and efficiently. This can enable greater collaboration between healthcare providers, resulting in better patient outcomes.

By using blockchain, healthcare providers can create an immutable record of patient data, which can help to prevent data breaches and protect patient privacy. This can be particularly important for sensitive medical information, such as mental health records or genetic data.

One example of a company using blockchain for healthcare is Medicalchain, a UK-based startup that is developing a blockchain-based platform for electronic health records. The platform allows patients to access and control their own health records, and can enable greater collaboration between healthcare providers.

Another example is the partnership between the US Department of Health and Human Services (HHS) and IBM, which is exploring the use of blockchain for secure and efficient data sharing in the healthcare industry.

Overall, the cloud and blockchain can provide significant benefits for the healthcare industry, including increased security, efficiency, and collaboration. As more healthcare providers adopt these technologies, we can expect to see greater innovation and disruption in the healthcare industry.

Real Estate

The real estate industry is another area that can benefit from the cloud and blockchain. By leveraging the cloud, real estate professionals can store and share property data more securely and efficiently. This can enable greater transparency and accountability, resulting in better transactions for both buyers and sellers.

By using blockchain, real estate professionals can create an immutable record of property data, including ownership records, transaction history, and other relevant information. This can help to prevent fraud and errors, and can provide greater transparency for buyers and sellers.

One example of a company using blockchain for real estate is Propy, a California-based startup that is developing a blockchain-based platform for real estate transactions. The platform enables buyers and sellers to complete real estate transactions using smart contracts, which can automate processes such as property transfer and payment.

Another example is the partnership between the government of the Republic of Georgia and the Bitfury Group, which has developed a blockchain-based platform for property registration. The platform enables property owners to register their property using blockchain, providing greater security and transparency for property ownership.

Overall, the cloud and blockchain can provide significant benefits for the real estate industry, including increased security, transparency, and efficiency. As more real estate professionals adopt these technologies, we can expect to see greater innovation and disruption in the real estate industry.

Conclusion

The cloud and blockchain are two of the most important technologies of our time, and they have the potential to transform many industries. By leveraging the power of the cloud and the security of blockchain, businesses can achieve greater efficiency, cost savings, and innovation.

In conclusion, the cloud and blockchain are not competing technologies, but rather complementary ones. Together, they can offer businesses a powerful toolset for achieving their goals and driving growth. As more businesses explore these technologies and integrate them into their operations, we can expect to see continued innovation and disruption in many industries. It is important for businesses to stay up to date with the latest developments in both the cloud and blockchain, and to be proactive in leveraging these technologies to create value for their customers and stakeholders.

Blockchain and Gaming

Gaming has always been at the forefront of technological innovation. As the gaming industry has grown, it has become an increasingly attractive target for blockchain developers. Blockchain has the potential to revolutionize the gaming industry by introducing new models of ownership, security, and player engagement.

What is Blockchain Gaming?

Blockchain gaming is a new form of gaming that uses blockchain technology to create decentralized gaming platforms. In a traditional game, the player owns the game assets and the developer owns the game platform. In a blockchain game, the player owns the assets and the platform is owned by the community.

Blockchain gaming is built on a decentralized platform that uses smart contracts to govern game mechanics, transactions, and other aspects of gameplay. Smart contracts are self-executing contracts that are stored on the blockchain. They are designed to automatically execute the terms of the contract when certain conditions are met.

The decentralized nature of blockchain gaming creates a more transparent and fair gaming environment. It enables players to own and control their assets, and it reduces the risk of fraud and cheating. Blockchain gaming also provides players with greater flexibility and mobility, as they can use their assets across multiple games and platforms.

How Does Blockchain Gaming Work?

Blockchain gaming is built on a blockchain platform that uses smart contracts to manage game mechanics, transactions, and other aspects of gameplay. Players can use cryptocurrencies or other digital assets to buy and sell game assets, and they can earn rewards for playing the game.

In a blockchain game, each asset is represented by a unique token that is stored on the blockchain. The token contains all the information about the asset, including its ownership, value, and history. This enables players to buy, sell, and trade assets without the need for a centralized intermediary.

Smart contracts are used to manage game mechanics, such as the rules of the game, the distribution of rewards, and the execution of transactions. They are also used to manage player interactions, such as the creation of teams, the management of competitions, and the resolution of disputes.

Blockchain gaming platforms also use decentralized storage to store game data, such as player scores, game history, and other information. This provides a more secure and transparent way of storing data, as it reduces the risk of data loss or tampering.

What Are the Benefits of Blockchain Gaming?

There are several benefits of blockchain gaming, including:

Ownership: In a blockchain game, players own their assets and have complete control over them. This provides players with greater flexibility and mobility, as they can use their assets across multiple games and platforms.

Security: Blockchain gaming provides a more secure and transparent gaming environment. It reduces the risk of fraud and cheating, as all transactions are recorded on the blockchain.

Fairness: Blockchain gaming creates a more transparent and fair gaming environment. It reduces the risk of bias and favoritism, as all transactions are recorded on the blockchain.

Interoperability: Blockchain gaming enables players to use their assets across multiple games and platforms. This provides players with greater flexibility and mobility.

Rewards: Blockchain gaming provides players with new ways to earn rewards for playing the game. Players can earn rewards for completing quests, participating in competitions, and other activities.

What Are the Challenges of Blockchain Gaming?

While blockchain gaming has many benefits, it also faces several challenges, including:

User adoption: Blockchain gaming is still a relatively new concept, and many players are not yet familiar with the technology. This can make it difficult to attract new players and build a large user base.

Complexity: Blockchain gaming can be more complex than traditional gaming, as it requires players to manage their own assets and transactions. This can be challenging for players who are not familiar with cryptocurrencies or blockchain technology.

Scalability: Blockchain gaming can be slower and less scalable than traditional gaming, as all transactions must be verified by the network of nodes. As the number of users and transactions grows, the blockchain can become congested, leading to slower transaction times and higher fees.

Regulatory uncertainty: The regulatory environment for blockchain gaming is still unclear in many jurisdictions, which can create legal and financial risks for developers and players.

Despite these challenges, blockchain gaming has a bright future ahead. As more players become familiar with the technology and more developers create innovative games, blockchain gaming has the potential to transform the gaming industry and create new opportunities for players and developers alike.

In summary, blockchain technology has the potential to revolutionize the gaming industry by increasing transparency, security, and ownership of in-game assets. Blockchain gaming enables players to earn real value from their gaming experiences, creating a new paradigm in the gaming industry. While the technology is still in its early stages, the potential for blockchain gaming is enormous, and we are excited to see how it will evolve in the years to come.

Supply Chain Management and Blockchain

Supply chain management is a critical component of modern business operations. It involves coordinating the flow of goods, services, and information from the source of production to the final consumer. Supply chains are complex and involve many different parties, including suppliers, manufacturers, distributors, and retailers. The efficient and effective management of these supply chains is essential to the success of any business.

One of the biggest challenges in supply chain management is the lack of transparency and visibility. As supply chains become more global and complex, it becomes increasingly difficult to track the movement of goods and ensure that they meet the required standards. This lack of transparency can lead to a variety of issues, including counterfeiting, theft, and fraud.

Blockchain technology has emerged as a potential solution to these challenges. Blockchain is a distributed ledger technology that enables the creation of a secure, tamper-proof, and transparent record of all transactions. By using blockchain technology in supply chain management, businesses can create a shared, real-time view of the entire supply chain, from raw materials to finished products. This can enable greater transparency and accountability, as businesses can track the movement of goods and materials at every stage of the supply chain.

How Does Blockchain Work in Supply Chain Management?

The basic idea behind using blockchain technology in supply chain management is to create a shared, immutable, and transparent record of all transactions in the supply chain. This record is stored on a decentralized network of computers, which makes it difficult for any single party to manipulate or control the data. In this way, blockchain technology can enable greater transparency, accountability, and efficiency in supply chain management.

There are several different ways in which blockchain can be used in supply chain management. One of the most common use cases is to track the movement of goods and materials through the supply chain. By using blockchain technology to create an immutable record of each transaction in the supply chain, businesses can create a transparent and tamper-proof record of the movement of goods and materials. This can help to prevent counterfeiting, theft, and fraud, and can enable businesses to quickly and easily identify any issues in the supply chain.

Another way in which blockchain can be used in supply chain management is to create a shared, real-time view of the entire supply chain. By using blockchain technology to create a shared database of all transactions in the supply chain, businesses can ensure that everyone in the supply chain has access to the same information. This can enable greater collaboration, efficiency, and transparency in the supply chain, as all parties can work together to identify and resolve any issues.

Finally, blockchain can be used to automate certain processes in the supply chain. By using smart contracts, businesses can create self-executing contracts that automatically trigger certain actions when certain conditions are met. For example, a smart contract could be used to automatically trigger the payment of an invoice when a shipment is delivered. This can help to streamline the supply chain and reduce the need for manual intervention.

Benefits of Using Blockchain in Supply Chain Management

There are several key benefits to using blockchain technology in supply chain management. These include:

Greater transparency and accountability: By using blockchain technology to create a shared, tamper-proof record of all transactions in the supply chain, businesses can create greater transparency and accountability. This can help to prevent counterfeiting, theft, and fraud, and can enable businesses to quickly identify and resolve any issues in the supply chain.

Improved efficiency and collaboration: By creating a shared, real-time view of the entire supply chain, businesses can improve collaboration and efficiency. All parties in the supply chain can work together to identify and resolve any issues, and can quickly adapt to any changes in the supply chain.

Reduced costs: By automating certain processes in the supply chain, businesses can reduce the need for manual intervention and reduce costs. Smart contracts can be used to automatically trigger payments, verify quality control, and even monitor inventory levels to ensure efficient production.

Enhanced transparency and traceability: One of the most significant advantages of blockchain in supply chain management is the increased transparency and traceability it offers. With blockchain, all transactions are recorded and stored in an immutable ledger that can be accessed and audited by all parties involved in the supply chain. This enables greater accountability and trust among suppliers, manufacturers, and retailers, as each party can track the movement of goods and materials at every stage of the supply chain.

Improved efficiency and speed: By digitizing the supply chain and reducing the need for manual intervention, blockchain can improve the speed and efficiency of supply chain processes. This can enable businesses to reduce lead times, respond more quickly to changes in demand, and improve overall supply chain performance.

Reduced risk of fraud and errors: With blockchain, all transactions are cryptographically secured and stored on a distributed ledger, reducing the risk of fraud and errors. This can be particularly valuable in high-value transactions or in industries with a high risk of fraud, such as the pharmaceutical or luxury goods industries.

Despite these potential benefits, there are also several challenges and limitations to the use of blockchain in supply chain management:

Interoperability: One of the key challenges facing the adoption of blockchain in supply chain management is the lack of interoperability between different blockchain platforms. As there are currently no universal standards for blockchain, this can make it difficult to integrate different blockchain platforms and ensure that all parties in the supply chain are using the same system.

Scalability: Another challenge facing the adoption of blockchain in supply chain management is scalability. As the number of transactions in the supply chain increases, the blockchain network can become slower and less efficient, leading to delays and increased costs.

Cost: While blockchain can ultimately reduce costs in the supply chain, the initial investment required to implement a blockchain solution can be high. This can be a significant barrier to entry for small and medium-sized businesses, particularly those in developing countries.

Regulatory challenges: Another challenge facing the adoption of blockchain in supply chain management is the lack of clear regulatory frameworks. As blockchain is a relatively new technology, there are few established regulations governing its use in supply chain management, which can make it difficult for businesses to ensure compliance and avoid legal challenges.

In spite of these challenges, the use of blockchain in supply chain management is growing rapidly, with a number of high-profile companies, including Walmart, Nestle, and Maersk, already implementing blockchain solutions in their supply chains. As blockchain technology continues to mature and become more widely adopted, it is likely that we will see an increasing number of businesses turning to blockchain to improve the efficiency, transparency, and security of their supply chains.

Blockchain Technology and Quality Assurance

Quality assurance is an essential component of any manufacturing or service industry. It involves the process of ensuring that products or services meet the required quality standards before they are delivered to the end-users. Traditionally, quality assurance has been a manual process that involves a lot of paperwork, manual tracking, and time-consuming audits. However, with the advent of blockchain technology, there is a potential for revolutionizing quality assurance. Blockchain technology can help businesses achieve greater transparency, traceability, and accountability, which are essential for ensuring quality in products and services. In this chapter, we will explore the potential of blockchain technology in quality assurance.

The Challenges of Traditional Quality Assurance:

Traditional quality assurance processes involve a lot of paperwork, manual tracking, and time-consuming audits. The lack of transparency and traceability in traditional quality assurance processes can lead to errors, fraud, and other malpractices. It can also make it difficult to identify the source of defects or quality issues, leading to delays in addressing the problems. Furthermore, traditional quality assurance processes can be slow, inefficient, and expensive, especially when dealing with complex supply chains that involve multiple stakeholders.

How Blockchain Technology Can Help:

Blockchain technology can help address many of the challenges of traditional quality assurance processes. By leveraging blockchain technology, businesses can create a shared, immutable, and tamper-proof ledger that records all the transactions and activities in the quality assurance process. This can help increase transparency, traceability, and accountability, which are essential for ensuring quality in products and services. Here are some ways that blockchain technology can help in quality assurance:

Immutable Record-Keeping:

Blockchain technology can help create an immutable record of all the transactions and activities in the quality assurance process. This can include everything from raw material sourcing to final product delivery. The ledger is shared among all the stakeholders in the supply chain, and all the data is stored in a decentralized network. This ensures that the data is tamper-proof, and any attempt to alter or delete the data is immediately visible to all the stakeholders in the network. This creates an auditable and transparent record of the entire quality assurance process.

Real-Time Tracking:

Blockchain technology can enable real-time tracking of products and services throughout the supply chain. This can help businesses identify quality issues, defects, or other problems at an early stage, which can be critical in addressing them before they become significant issues. With blockchain, businesses can track the movement of goods and materials at every stage of the supply chain. This can include everything from raw material sourcing to final product delivery. Blockchain can also provide real-time alerts and notifications if any quality issues are detected.

Improved Transparency:

Blockchain technology can help increase transparency in quality assurance processes. With blockchain, businesses can create a shared, real-time view of the entire supply chain. This can include everything from raw material sourcing to final product delivery. By providing all the stakeholders with access to the same data, businesses can increase transparency and accountability in the quality assurance process. This can also help build trust between the different stakeholders in the supply chain.

Smart Contracts:

Smart contracts are self-executing contracts that can be programmed to automatically trigger specific actions based on pre-defined rules and conditions. Smart contracts can be used in quality assurance processes to automate certain processes, such as the approval of quality standards, tracking of products, and payments. This can help reduce the need for manual intervention and increase the efficiency of the quality assurance process.

Improved Efficiency:

Blockchain technology can help improve the efficiency of quality assurance processes. With blockchain, businesses can automate many of the manual processes that are involved in quality assurance, such as data entry, tracking, and auditing. This can help reduce the time and costs involved in the quality assurance process. Furthermore, blockchain can enable real-time tracking of products and services, which can help businesses identify quality issues faster and take corrective actions immediately. This can result in a reduction in defects, recalls, and warranty claims, which can have a significant impact on a business's bottom line.

Increased Transparency:

Blockchain can bring greater transparency to the quality assurance process by providing a tamper-proof and immutable record of all quality-related data, including test results, inspections, and certifications. This can help businesses ensure that their products and services meet the required quality standards and comply with regulations. In addition, blockchain can enable suppliers to share their quality-related data with their customers, which can help build trust and transparency in the supply chain.

Traceability:

Traceability is a critical component of quality assurance, as it enables businesses to track the movement of products and services throughout the supply chain. With blockchain, businesses can create a permanent and transparent record of all product-related data, including its origin, manufacturing processes, and distribution. This can help businesses identify the root cause of quality issues and take corrective actions more quickly. In addition, blockchain can enable businesses to track the authenticity of products and prevent counterfeit goods from entering the supply chain.

Smart Contracts:

Smart contracts are self-executing contracts that are encoded on a blockchain. They can be used to automate quality-related processes, such as inspections, testing, and certifications. Smart contracts can help reduce the time and costs involved in quality assurance by eliminating the need for manual intervention. For example, a smart contract can automatically trigger an inspection when a product is received, and only release the product if it passes the inspection.

Challenges:

Despite the many benefits of blockchain technology in quality assurance, there are several challenges that need to be addressed. These include:

Integration: Integrating blockchain technology with existing quality management systems can be challenging, as it requires significant changes to the existing processes and systems. Businesses need to carefully plan and execute the integration process to ensure that it is done effectively.

Data standardization: Ensuring data standardization is critical for blockchain to be effective in quality assurance. All parties involved in the supply chain need to agree on a set of data standards and definitions to ensure that the data is consistent and accurate.

Regulatory compliance: Blockchain technology is still largely unregulated, and there is a lack of clarity on how it fits into existing regulations. This can create uncertainty and legal challenges for businesses that use blockchain in quality assurance.

Conclusion:
Blockchain technology has the potential to revolutionize the way quality assurance is conducted in businesses across industries. By improving efficiency, increasing transparency, enabling traceability, and using smart contracts, blockchain can help businesses reduce costs, improve product quality, and comply with regulations. However, businesses need to carefully plan and execute the integration process and address the challenges associated with the technology to fully realize its potential.

CHAPTER 13 - PROOF OF WORK VS. PROOF OF STAKE

What is Proof of Work?
What is Proof of Stake?
Benefits of the Proof of Stake Model
Proof of Stake Challenges
BLOCKCHAIN SECRETS

Proof of work is a consensus algorithm that has been used in blockchain technology since its inception. It is used to validate transactions, create new blocks, and secure the network. In this chapter, we will explore what proof of work is, how it works, and its advantages and disadvantages. We will also compare proof of work to other consensus algorithms, such as proof of stake, and discuss the future of proof of work in blockchain technology.

What is Proof of Work?

In the world of blockchain technology, one of the most important concepts is proof of work. Proof of work is a consensus algorithm used to confirm transactions and create new blocks in a blockchain. It was first introduced by Bitcoin, the world's first decentralized cryptocurrency. In this chapter, we'll dive into what proof of work is, how it works, and its advantages and disadvantages.

What is Proof of Work?

Proof of work is a consensus algorithm that is used in blockchain technology to verify and validate transactions. In a blockchain network, transactions are verified by a group of nodes called miners. Miners use their computing power to solve complex mathematical problems, which confirm transactions and create new blocks in the blockchain.

In the proof of work system, the miners compete with each other to solve these mathematical problems. The first miner to solve the problem gets to add the new block to the blockchain and receive a reward in the form of cryptocurrency. This process is known as mining.

How Does Proof of Work Work?

To understand how proof of work works, let's take a closer look at the mining process. When a new transaction is submitted to the network, it is broadcasted to all the nodes in the network. Each node checks the transaction to make sure it is valid, and then broadcasts it to other nodes. Eventually, the transaction reaches the miners, who add it to a pool of unconfirmed transactions.

To add a new block to the blockchain, the miners must solve a complex mathematical problem. The problem is designed to be difficult to solve, but easy to verify once it has been solved. The problem requires a significant amount of computational power to solve, which is why miners compete to solve it.

The first miner to solve the problem broadcasts the solution to the network, and the other nodes in the network verify the solution. If the solution is valid, the miner is rewarded with cryptocurrency and the new block is added to the blockchain.

The difficulty of the mathematical problem is adjusted based on the computing power of the network. The more computing power that is added to the network, the more difficult the problem becomes. This is done to ensure that blocks are created at a steady rate and that the network remains secure.

Advantages of Proof of Work

One of the main advantages of proof of work is its security. Because miners are competing to solve the mathematical problem, it is very difficult for any single miner to manipulate the network. In order to do so, the miner would need to control more than 50% of the network's computing power, which is known as a 51% attack. This is very difficult and expensive to do, which makes the network very secure.

Another advantage of proof of work is its decentralization. Because anyone can become a miner and participate in the network, there is no centralized authority that controls the network. This makes the network more resilient to attacks and more resistant to censorship.

Disadvantages of Proof of Work

While proof of work has many advantages, it also has some disadvantages. One of the main disadvantages is its energy consumption. Because mining requires a significant amount of computational power, it consumes a lot of energy. This has led to concerns about the environmental impact of cryptocurrencies like Bitcoin.

Another disadvantage of proof of work is its scalability. As more and more people join the network and start mining, the difficulty of the mathematical problem increases. This makes it more difficult and more expensive for new miners to join the network. This can limit the growth of the network and make it less accessible to new participants.

Conclusion

In conclusion, proof of work is a fundamental concept in blockchain technology. It is an important mechanism for validating transactions, creating new blocks, and securing the network. While it has some disadvantages such as high energy consumption, slow transaction processing times, and the potential for centralization, it remains the most widely used consensus algorithm in blockchain technology.

As blockchain technology continues to evolve, there are ongoing efforts to address the issues associated with proof of work, including the development of new consensus algorithms such as proof of stake, proof of authority, and delegated proof of stake. These alternative consensus algorithms have their own advantages and disadvantages, and their effectiveness will depend on the specific use case and requirements of the blockchain network.

Regardless of the consensus algorithm used, it is clear that blockchain technology has the potential to revolutionize industries and transform the way we conduct transactions, store data, and interact with each other. By providing a secure, transparent, and decentralized platform for conducting business, blockchain technology can help build trust and drive innovation across a wide range of applications, from finance and healthcare to supply chain management and gaming.

What is Proof of Stake?

In the world of blockchain, consensus algorithms are used to validate transactions and create new blocks. One of the most popular consensus algorithms is Proof of Work (PoW), which requires participants to solve complex mathematical problems in order to validate transactions and earn rewards. However, PoW has some limitations, such as high energy consumption and low scalability. To address these issues, a new consensus algorithm called Proof of Stake (PoS) was developed.

What is Proof of Stake?

Proof of Stake is a consensus algorithm that was first introduced in 2012 by a developer named Sunny King. Unlike PoW, which requires participants to solve complex mathematical problems, PoS requires participants to prove ownership of a certain amount of cryptocurrency in order to validate transactions and create new blocks.

The basic idea behind PoS is that the more cryptocurrency a participant holds, the more likely they are to be chosen to validate transactions and earn rewards. This is because PoS uses a random selection process called "coin age" to determine which participant is chosen to create the next block. Coin age is calculated based on the amount of cryptocurrency a participant holds and the length of time it has been held.

To participate in PoS, users need to hold a certain amount of cryptocurrency, which is known as a "stake." The amount of stake required to participate in PoS varies depending on the blockchain, but it is usually significantly lower than the amount of computational power required for PoW. This means that PoS is more energy-efficient and has lower barriers to entry compared to PoW.

Advantages of Proof of Stake

One of the main advantages of PoS is that it is more energy-efficient than PoW. Since PoS does not require participants to solve complex mathematical problems, it consumes much less energy than PoW. This is because the validation process in PoS is based on the amount of cryptocurrency a participant holds, rather than the amount of computational power they can provide.

Another advantage of PoS is that it has lower barriers to entry compared to PoW. Since PoS does not require participants to invest in expensive hardware, it is easier for individuals to participate in the network. This can help increase the decentralization of the network, which is a key goal of blockchain technology.

Finally, PoS can be more scalable than PoW. Since PoS does not require participants to solve complex mathematical problems, it can process transactions more quickly and handle a higher volume of transactions.

Disadvantages of Proof of Stake

Despite its advantages, PoS also has some disadvantages. One of the main concerns with PoS is the potential for centralization. Since PoS rewards participants based on the amount of cryptocurrency they hold, those who hold large amounts of cryptocurrency have a greater chance of being chosen to validate transactions and earn rewards. This can lead to a situation where a small number of participants control the majority of the network, which can undermine the decentralization of the network.

Another concern with PoS is the potential for "nothing at stake" attacks. In a PoS network, participants are not penalized for voting for multiple versions of the blockchain. This means that a malicious participant could potentially vote for multiple versions of the blockchain without penalty, which could result in a network fork.

Finally, PoS requires a certain level of trust in the participants. Since the validation process is based on the amount of cryptocurrency a participant holds, there is a risk that a large participant could collude with others to manipulate the network.

Conclusion

Proof of Stake is a consensus algorithm that is gaining popularity in the world of blockchain. It offers several advantages over PoW, including lower energy consumption, lower barriers to entry, and greater scalability. However, it also has some potential disadvantages, such as the risk of centralization and "nothing at stake" attacks.

Benefits of the Proof of Stake Model

The Proof of Stake (PoS) model is a consensus algorithm used in blockchain technology to validate transactions and create new blocks. It differs from the Proof of Work (PoW) model in that it does not rely on computational power and electricity consumption to secure the network. Instead, PoS uses a different mechanism that rewards users for holding and staking their cryptocurrency. In this chapter, we will explore the benefits of the Proof of Stake model.

Energy Efficiency

One of the main benefits of PoS over PoW is energy efficiency. In the PoW model, miners compete to solve complex mathematical problems, which requires a significant amount of computational power and energy consumption. This energy consumption has become a growing concern in recent years, with some estimates suggesting that the Bitcoin network alone consumes as much energy as the entire country of Argentina.

In contrast, PoS does not require such a high level of energy consumption. Instead, validators (also called "stakers") are chosen to create new blocks based on the amount of cryptocurrency they hold and are willing to "stake" or lock up in the network. This means that PoS networks can achieve the same level of security as PoW networks with significantly less energy consumption.

Decentralization

Another benefit of PoS is that it can help to promote decentralization. In a PoW network, the majority of the mining power can be concentrated in the hands of a few large mining pools or corporations. This can lead to concerns around centralization and potential attacks on the network.

In contrast, PoS networks are designed to promote decentralization by incentivizing users to hold and stake their cryptocurrency. This means that the network is secured by a larger number of users, rather than a few large miners. Additionally, PoS networks often have mechanisms in place to prevent large validators from accumulating too much power and potentially harming the network.

Security

PoS networks can also provide a high level of security. In a PoS network, validators are required to stake their own cryptocurrency in order to participate in the network. This means that they have a financial stake in ensuring that the network remains secure and operational. If a validator is found to be acting maliciously, they can lose their staked cryptocurrency.

Additionally, PoS networks often have mechanisms in place to incentivize good behavior and punish bad behavior. For example, some PoS networks allow users to "vote" on which validators they trust, and the validators with the most votes are chosen to create new blocks. This means that validators are incentivized to act in the best interests of the network and its users.

Scalability

PoS networks can also be more scalable than PoW networks. In a PoW network, the block size is limited by the amount of computational power available to miners. This means that as the network grows, the time it takes to validate transactions and create new blocks can increase significantly.

In a PoS network, the block size is not limited by computational power. Instead, validators are chosen based on the amount of cryptocurrency they hold and are willing to stake. This means that PoS networks can potentially process more transactions per second than PoW networks, which can help to improve scalability.

Accessibility

Finally, PoS networks can be more accessible than PoW networks. In a PoW network, mining requires a significant investment in hardware and electricity. This can make it difficult for individuals to participate in the network.

In contrast, PoS networks only require users to hold and stake cryptocurrency. This means that individuals with smaller amounts of cryptocurrency can participate in the network and potentially earn rewards for validating transactions and creating new blocks.

In conclusion, the Proof of Stake model has several benefits over the Proof of Work model. It is more energy-efficient, promotes decentralization, provides a high levelof security, and is more accessible to a wider range of individuals. As blockchain technology continues to evolve and become more mainstream, it is likely that we will see more adoption of the PoS model in various blockchain networks.

One area where the PoS model is particularly well-suited is in the development of decentralized finance (DeFi) platforms. DeFi platforms use blockchain technology to create financial services and applications that are accessible to anyone with an internet connection, without the need for traditional financial intermediaries such as banks. The PoS model is particularly beneficial for DeFi platforms, as it enables individuals to participate in network validation and governance, and potentially earn rewards for doing so.

Overall, the Proof of Stake model represents an important innovation in blockchain technology. By providing a more energy-efficient, secure, and accessible consensus mechanism, PoS networks have the potential to drive greater adoption of blockchain technology and enable new use cases and applications. As the technology continues to mature, it will be interesting to see how the PoS model evolves and is applied in various blockchain networks and industries.

Proof of Stake Challenges

Proof of Stake (PoS) is a consensus mechanism in blockchain technology that allows validators to create new blocks and validate transactions based on the amount of cryptocurrency they hold and stake. While PoS offers several benefits over the Proof of Work (PoW) model, it also faces several challenges that must be addressed.

One of the biggest challenges facing PoS networks is the issue of centralization. In a PoS network, validators are chosen based on the amount of cryptocurrency they hold and stake. This means that individuals or organizations with a large amount of cryptocurrency can become dominant validators and have significant control over the network. This can lead to a lack of decentralization, which can undermine the security and reliability of the network.

To address this challenge, some PoS networks have implemented measures to promote decentralization, such as limiting the amount of cryptocurrency that a single validator can hold and stake. Additionally, some networks have implemented random selection processes to choose validators, which can help prevent a small group of validators from dominating the network.

Another challenge facing PoS networks is the issue of security. While PoS networks are more energy-efficient than PoW networks, they are still vulnerable to certain types of attacks, such as a "51% attack." In a 51% attack, a single validator or group of validators controls the majority of the network's staked cryptocurrency, giving them the ability to manipulate transactions and potentially double-spend cryptocurrency.

To address this challenge, some PoS networks have implemented measures to prevent 51% attacks, such as requiring validators to have a certain amount of cryptocurrency staked or implementing penalties for malicious behavior. Additionally, some networks have implemented a "slashing" mechanism, which punishes validators who engage in malicious behavior by confiscating a portion of their staked cryptocurrency.

Another challenge facing PoS networks is the issue of network latency. In a PoS network, validators must communicate with each other to validate transactions and create new blocks. This communication can be slow, especially as the network grows and more validators are added. This can lead to longer block times and slower transaction processing speeds, which can impact the usability and scalability of the network.

To address this challenge, some PoS networks have implemented measures to improve network latency, such as implementing sharding or sidechain solutions to reduce the amount of data that needs to be processed by validators. Additionally, some networks have implemented mechanisms to incentivize validators to process transactions quickly, such as providing rewards for validators who process a certain number of transactions within a set time frame.

Finally, another challenge facing PoS networks is the issue of network governance. In a PoS network, validators have a significant amount of control over the network, which can make it difficult to implement changes or upgrades to the network. Additionally, validators may have conflicting interests or agendas, which can make it difficult to reach consensus on important issues.

To address this challenge, some PoS networks have implemented mechanisms for network governance, such as voting systems or proposal processes, which allow validators to vote on changes or upgrades to the network. Additionally, some networks have implemented mechanisms to incentivize validators to act in the best interests of the network, such as providing rewards for validators who propose and implement beneficial changes to the network.

In conclusion, while the Proof of Stake model offers several benefits over the Proof of Work model, it also faces several challenges that must be addressed. These challenges include centralization, security, network latency, and network governance. As PoS networks continue to evolve and grow, it will be important for developers and stakeholders to address these challenges to ensure the long-term viability and success of the networks.

BLOCKCHAIN SECRETS

Blockchain Secrets: Understanding the Importance of Privacy and Confidentiality in Blockchain Technology

Blockchain technology has become increasingly popular in recent years, providing innovative solutions to various industries, from finance to healthcare. However, one of the most significant challenges that blockchain technology faces is the issue of privacy and confidentiality. While blockchain technology is designed to be transparent and secure, the open and decentralized nature of the technology has made it difficult to ensure that sensitive information is protected.

In this chapter, we will explore the importance of privacy and confidentiality in blockchain technology, and how these concepts can be addressed to ensure the continued growth and success of the technology.

The Importance of Privacy and Confidentiality in Blockchain Technology

Privacy and confidentiality are crucial components of any system that handles sensitive information. In blockchain technology, privacy refers to the ability to keep transactions and data hidden from unauthorized parties, while confidentiality refers to the ability to ensure that sensitive data is only accessible by authorized parties.

The lack of privacy and confidentiality in blockchain technology can have serious consequences, such as the exposure of personal or confidential information, financial loss, or even reputational damage. It is, therefore, essential that privacy and confidentiality are addressed in any blockchain implementation.

Blockchain technology is often associated with anonymity and pseudonymity, which can provide users with a sense of privacy. However, this anonymity can also be a double-edged sword, as it can be used to facilitate illegal activities, such as money laundering or terrorist financing.

To address these challenges, various privacy and confidentiality solutions have been developed for blockchain technology.

Privacy and Confidentiality Solutions in Blockchain Technology

One solution to the privacy and confidentiality challenges in blockchain technology is the use of private or permissioned blockchains. Private blockchains are closed systems that only allow authorized parties to participate, while permissioned blockchains restrict access to certain functions or data to specific users.

Another solution is the use of cryptographic techniques, such as zero-knowledge proofs or ring signatures. These techniques enable parties to prove their identity or knowledge of certain information without revealing the information itself, ensuring that sensitive data remains confidential.

Additionally, several projects have focused on developing privacy-focused cryptocurrencies, such as Monero or Zcash. These cryptocurrencies use various techniques, such as ring signatures or zk-SNARKs, to obscure transaction data and provide users with a high level of privacy.

Challenges to Implementing Privacy and Confidentiality Solutions

While privacy and confidentiality solutions have been developed for blockchain technology, there are still several challenges to their implementation.

One of the main challenges is the tension between privacy and transparency. Blockchain technology was designed to be transparent, allowing anyone to view transaction data and verify the integrity of the network. However, this transparency can be at odds with the need for privacy and confidentiality. Finding the right balance between transparency and privacy is, therefore, crucial to the success of any blockchain implementation.

Another challenge is the scalability of privacy-focused solutions. Cryptographic techniques, such as zero-knowledge proofs, can be computationally intensive, which can slow down transaction processing times and limit the scalability of the network. This can be particularly problematic for public blockchains, where thousands of transactions can occur per second.

Furthermore, the use of privacy-focused solutions can make it difficult for regulatory authorities to monitor and regulate the network. This can be a significant barrier to the adoption of blockchain technology, particularly in industries where strict regulatory compliance is required.

Conclusion

Privacy and confidentiality are critical components of any system that handles sensitive information, and blockchain technology is no exception. While the transparent and decentralized nature of blockchain technology has made it difficult to ensure privacy and confidentiality, various solutions have been developed to address these challenges.

As blockchain technology continues to evolve, privacy and confidentiality will remain crucial to its continued growth and success. Finding the right balance between transparency and privacy and addressing scalability and regulatory challenges will be essential to the widespread adoption of blockchain technology. The development of new technologies such as zero-knowledge proofs, multi-party computation, and secure enclaves will help to address these challenges and enhance the privacy and confidentiality of blockchain networks.

In addition to technical solutions, there is also a need for regulatory frameworks that can support the growth of blockchain technology while ensuring privacy and confidentiality. Governments and regulatory bodies must balance the need for innovation and growth with the protection of consumers and the prevention of illegal activities. Collaborative efforts between the blockchain industry and regulatory bodies can help to create a regulatory environment that supports innovation while ensuring privacy and confidentiality.

Overall, privacy and confidentiality are critical components of blockchain technology that must be addressed to ensure its continued growth and success. As blockchain technology continues to evolve and new solutions are developed, it is likely that we will see a more widespread adoption of blockchain technology across a range of industries and use cases.

CHAPTER 14 - BENEFITS OF BLOCKCHAIN TECHNOLOGY

Eliminating Third Parties
Control Over Data
Better Data Quality and Integrity
Durability and Reliability
The Integrity of Data Processing and Transfers
Transparency and Auditability
Faster Transactions
Lower Transaction Costs

In traditional systems, data processing and transfer can be complicated, time-consuming, and costly. These systems often involve third-party intermediaries, resulting in a lack of control over data and increased transaction costs. However, with the emergence of blockchain technology, organizations are now able to streamline data processing and transfer, eliminate third parties, and reduce transaction costs. In this chapter, we will explore how blockchain technology enables better control over data, improves data quality and integrity, provides greater transparency and auditability, and facilitates faster and cheaper transactions. We will also discuss some of the challenges that come with implementing blockchain technology in data processing and transfer, as well as some of the potential solutions to overcome these challenges.

Eliminating Third Parties

Blockchain technology has the potential to disrupt many industries by eliminating the need for trusted third parties. In traditional systems, trusted third parties are responsible for verifying and processing transactions, and they often charge significant fees for their services. However, blockchain technology allows for trust to be established through the use of cryptography and decentralized networks, which can eliminate the need for third parties.

Eliminating third parties has numerous benefits, including reduced costs, increased efficiency, and greater security. In this chapter, we will explore the ways in which blockchain technology can be used to eliminate third parties in various industries.

Decentralized Finance (DeFi)

One of the most promising use cases for eliminating third parties with blockchain technology is in the realm of decentralized finance (DeFi). DeFi is a system of financial applications built on blockchain technology that allow for peer-to-peer transactions without the need for intermediaries such as banks or other financial institutions.

DeFi applications use smart contracts to execute financial transactions automatically and transparently on the blockchain. This eliminates the need for intermediaries such as banks, which can significantly reduce costs and increase efficiency. Additionally, since transactions are executed automatically by smart contracts, there is no risk of human error or fraud.

Real Estate

Another industry that could benefit from the elimination of third parties with blockchain technology is real estate. In traditional real estate transactions, numerous intermediaries are involved, including real estate agents, title companies, and banks. These intermediaries often charge significant fees, which can make buying or selling property prohibitively expensive.

Blockchain technology can be used to create a transparent and secure system for real estate transactions, eliminating the need for intermediaries. Smart contracts can be used to automate the transfer of ownership and payment, reducing the risk of fraud or errors. Additionally, blockchain technology can enable fractional ownership, which can make real estate investment more accessible to a wider range of individuals.

Supply Chain Management

Blockchain technology can also be used to eliminate third parties in supply chain management. In traditional supply chain systems, numerous intermediaries are involved in the movement of goods, including freight forwarders, customs brokers, and insurers. These intermediaries can increase costs and add complexity to the supply chain.

By using blockchain technology, supply chain management can become more efficient and cost-effective. Smart contracts can be used to automate processes such as customs clearance and insurance claims, reducing the need for intermediaries. Additionally, the transparency of the blockchain can help to reduce fraud and improve traceability, which can increase trust and reduce risk.

Conclusion

Eliminating third parties is one of the most promising use cases for blockchain technology. By using cryptography and decentralized networks to establish trust, blockchain technology can eliminate the need for intermediaries in various industries, including finance, real estate, and supply chain management. This can reduce costs, increase efficiency, and improve security and transparency. As blockchain technology continues to evolve, we can expect to see more industries adopt this technology and reap the benefits of eliminating third parties

Control Over Data

Blockchain technology offers several benefits, including transparency, security, and decentralization. One of the most significant benefits of blockchain is the ability to provide individuals and businesses with control over their data.

Traditionally, data has been controlled by centralized entities such as governments and corporations. This has led to concerns over data privacy and security, as well as a lack of control for individuals over their personal data. With blockchain technology, however, individuals and businesses can regain control over their data and determine how it is used and shared.

One way that blockchain technology provides control over data is through the use of private keys. Private keys are used to access and control cryptocurrency wallets, but they can also be used to control access to other types of data on the blockchain. By holding the private key, individuals and businesses can determine who has access to their data and how it is used.

Blockchain technology also allows for the creation of smart contracts, which are self-executing contracts with the terms of the agreement directly written into code on the blockchain. Smart contracts can be used to facilitate the exchange of data and ensure that data is only accessed or used according to the terms agreed upon by the parties involved.

Another way that blockchain technology provides control over data is through the use of decentralized storage. Decentralized storage networks allow individuals and businesses to store their data on the blockchain in a secure and distributed manner. This means that there is no central point of control for the data, and individuals and businesses can control who has access to it.

Decentralized storage also offers improved security, as the data is stored on multiple nodes on the blockchain rather than in a central location that is vulnerable to hacking and cyber attacks. Additionally, decentralized storage allows for greater privacy, as individuals and businesses can control who has access to their data and keep it separate from other data on the blockchain.

Overall, blockchain technology offers significant benefits when it comes to control over data. By utilizing private keys, smart contracts, and decentralized storage, individuals and businesses can regain control over their data and ensure that it is used and shared in a way that aligns with their values and goals.

In conclusion, blockchain technology has the potential to revolutionize the way that data is controlled and managed. By providing individuals and businesses with greater control over their data, blockchain technology can improve privacy, security, and transparency. As blockchain technology continues to evolve, we can expect to see even more innovative solutions for data control and management on the blockchain.

Better Data Quality and Integrity

Data is an essential aspect of every business and organization. It is used to make informed decisions, understand market trends, and improve customer experiences. However, the accuracy and integrity of data can be compromised in various ways, such as human error, system failures, and cyber attacks. Blockchain technology offers a solution to these challenges by providing better data quality and integrity. In this chapter, we will explore how blockchain technology can improve data quality and integrity and the benefits of this improvement.

What is Data Quality and Integrity?

Data quality refers to the accuracy, completeness, consistency, and timeliness of data. Data integrity refers to the trustworthiness, reliability, and consistency of data over time. These two concepts are closely related and are essential for organizations to make informed decisions and maintain customer trust.

However, maintaining data quality and integrity is not easy, and various challenges can compromise these aspects of data. For example, manual data entry can result in human error, leading to inaccurate data. System failures can also cause data loss or corruption, resulting in unreliable data. Cyber attacks can compromise the confidentiality and integrity of data, leading to data breaches and loss of trust.

How Blockchain Improves Data Quality and Integrity

Blockchain technology provides a decentralized, immutable, and transparent way of storing and sharing data. These characteristics offer several advantages for improving data quality and integrity.

Decentralized Storage: Traditional data storage methods rely on centralized servers that are vulnerable to attacks and system failures. Blockchain technology, on the other hand, uses a distributed network of nodes to store and validate data. This decentralized storage ensures that data is always available, even in the event of a system failure or cyber attack.

Immutable Data: Once data is added to a blockchain, it cannot be altered or deleted. This immutability ensures that the data is accurate and reliable, as it cannot be changed by a single party or authority.

Transparency: Blockchain technology provides a transparent way of storing and sharing data. Every transaction and change is recorded on the blockchain, and all network participants have access to the same information. This transparency ensures that data is consistent and trustworthy, as all parties have the same information.

Smart Contracts: Smart contracts are self-executing contracts that automatically enforce the rules and conditions of a transaction. They can be used to ensure that data is accurate and complete before it is added to the blockchain. This ensures that only high-quality data is added to the blockchain, improving data quality and integrity.

Benefits of Improved Data Quality and Integrity

Improved data quality and integrity offer several benefits for organizations and businesses.

Improved Decision Making: High-quality and reliable data are essential for making informed decisions. Improved data quality and integrity ensure that organizations have access to accurate and trustworthy data, leading to better decision-making processes.

Enhanced Customer Trust: Customers trust organizations that handle their data with care and accuracy. Improved data quality and integrity ensure that customer data is accurate and secure, leading to increased trust and loyalty.

Reduced Costs: Inaccurate or unreliable data can lead to increased costs, such as customer complaints, legal fees, and lost revenue. Improved data quality and integrity reduce these costs by ensuring that data is accurate and trustworthy, leading to better business outcomes.

Conclusion

Blockchain technology offers a promising solution to the challenges of maintaining data quality and integrity. By providing decentralized storage, immutability, transparency, and smart contracts, blockchain technology can ensure that data is accurate, reliable, and trustworthy. Improved data quality and integrity offer several benefits, including improved decision making, enhanced customer trust, and reduced costs. As blockchain technology continues to evolve, its role in improving data quality and integrity will become increasingly important.

Durability and Reliability

Blockchain technology is known for its durability and reliability, making it an attractive solution for businesses and organizations looking for a secure and robust system. Unlike traditional databases, which are centralized and vulnerable to various types of attacks and failures, blockchain technology is decentralized and provides a high level of data redundancy and fault tolerance. In this chapter, we will explore the durability and reliability of blockchain technology and the various features and characteristics that make it a reliable and secure system.

Durability of Blockchain Technology

One of the main benefits of blockchain technology is its durability. Blockchain technology is designed to store data in a decentralized manner, with multiple copies of the same data stored across a network of nodes. This means that even if some nodes fail or are compromised, the data can still be retrieved from other nodes in the network. This makes blockchain technology highly resistant to tampering and data loss.

The durability of blockchain technology is due to its distributed nature, which makes it difficult for any single entity to control or manipulate the network. Each node in the network has a copy of the blockchain, and all nodes work together to validate transactions and maintain the integrity of the network. As a result, any attempt to modify or manipulate the blockchain would require a majority of nodes to agree, which makes it almost impossible to tamper with the data.

Furthermore, blockchain technology uses cryptographic algorithms to ensure the integrity of data stored on the blockchain. Each block in the blockchain contains a hash, which is a unique digital fingerprint that represents the data in that block. If any part of the data in the block is changed, the hash will also change, alerting the network that the data has been tampered with. This makes it difficult for anyone to modify the data on the blockchain without being detected.

Reliability of Blockchain Technology

In addition to its durability, blockchain technology is also highly reliable. Blockchain networks are designed to operate 24/7, with nodes working together to validate transactions and maintain the network's integrity. This means that the network is always available, and transactions can be processed quickly and efficiently.

Moreover, blockchain technology is designed to be fault-tolerant, meaning that the network can continue to function even if some nodes fail or are taken offline. This is because each node in the network has a copy of the blockchain, and transactions can be validated by other nodes if some nodes are unavailable. This makes blockchain networks highly resistant to downtime and disruptions, ensuring that data and transactions are always available and accessible.

Another factor that contributes to the reliability of blockchain technology is the use of consensus mechanisms. Consensus mechanisms are algorithms used by blockchain networks to ensure that all nodes in the network agree on the state of the blockchain. This helps prevent forks or splits in the blockchain, which can lead to data inconsistencies and other issues.

Conclusion

The durability and reliability of blockchain technology make it an attractive solution for businesses and organizations looking for a secure and robust system. Blockchain technology's distributed nature, cryptographic algorithms, and fault-tolerant design make it highly resistant to tampering, data loss, and downtime. Additionally, the use of consensus mechanisms ensures that all nodes in the network agree on the state of the blockchain, preventing forks and data inconsistencies.

As blockchain technology continues to evolve, it is expected to become even more durable and reliable, with new features and improvements being introduced to enhance its security and performance. This makes blockchain technology an exciting area to watch, with many potential applications and use cases in a variety of industries and sectors.

The Integrity of Data Processing and Transfers

Blockchain technology has revolutionized the way data is processed and transferred, providing a more secure and efficient method compared to traditional systems. The use of distributed ledger technology has brought about numerous benefits to various industries, ranging from finance to healthcare and even supply chain management. One of the most significant benefits of blockchain technology is the integrity of data processing and transfers.

Traditionally, data processing and transfer systems have relied on centralized servers, which are vulnerable to attacks and system failures. This is due to the fact that centralized systems are managed by a single entity, making it easier for hackers to gain access to the system and manipulate the data. Additionally, centralized systems are also prone to human error, which can result in incorrect data being processed and transferred.

On the other hand, blockchain technology is based on a decentralized system, where data is stored on a distributed ledger that is maintained by a network of computers. Each computer on the network maintains a copy of the ledger, which ensures that the data is consistent and accurate. This eliminates the need for a single entity to manage the data, reducing the risk of cyberattacks and system failures.

The use of cryptography is also a crucial aspect of blockchain technology, providing an additional layer of security to the data. Each transaction on the blockchain is encrypted using complex mathematical algorithms, making it nearly impossible for hackers to tamper with the data. Additionally, blockchain technology provides transparency, allowing users to track the history of each transaction on the network.

Improved Data Integrity

One of the main benefits of blockchain technology is the improved data integrity. With the use of distributed ledger technology, data is stored on a decentralized network of computers, providing a more secure and tamper-proof method of data processing and transfer. Each transaction on the network is verified and validated by multiple nodes, ensuring that the data is consistent and accurate.

Furthermore, the use of cryptography provides an additional layer of security, making it virtually impossible for hackers to manipulate the data. Each transaction on the network is encrypted using complex mathematical algorithms, and once the transaction is recorded on the blockchain, it cannot be altered. This provides a high level of data integrity, ensuring that the data is accurate and trustworthy.

Reduced Risk of Human Error

Human error is a significant risk factor in data processing and transfer systems. Errors can occur due to various reasons, including miscommunication, misinterpretation of data, and manual data entry errors. These errors can result in incorrect data being processed and transferred, leading to serious consequences.

Blockchain technology eliminates the risk of human error by automating many of the processes involved in data processing and transfer. Smart contracts, for example, are self-executing contracts that are programmed to execute when certain conditions are met. This eliminates the need for manual intervention, reducing the risk of human error.

Improved Traceability and Auditability

Another benefit of blockchain technology is the improved traceability and auditability of data. With the use of distributed ledger technology, each transaction on the network is recorded and verified by multiple nodes. This provides a high level of transparency, allowing users to track the history of each transaction on the network.

This improved traceability and auditability can be particularly useful in industries such as supply chain management and healthcare. In the supply chain, blockchain technology can be used to track the movement of goods from the source to the end user, providing a transparent and auditable record of each transaction. In healthcare, blockchain technology can be used to securely store and share patient data, ensuring that the data is accurate and confidential.

Conclusion

The integrity of data processing and transfers is a crucial aspect of any system that handles sensitive information. Blockchain technology has revolutionized the way data is processed and transferred, providing a more secure and efficient method compared to traditional systems. The use of distributed ledger technology has brought about numerous benefits, including improved data integrity, reduced risk of human error , and increased transparency.

However, there are still challenges that need to be addressed to fully realize the potential of blockchain technology in ensuring the integrity of data processing and transfers. Some of these challenges include the need for scalable solutions to accommodate the increasing demand for data processing, the development of user-friendly interfaces for non-technical users, and the adoption of standardized protocols to ensure interoperability between different blockchain networks.

As the use cases for blockchain technology continue to expand, its impact on the integrity of data processing and transfers will only continue to grow. The benefits of blockchain technology will undoubtedly continue to be felt across various industries, including finance, healthcare, supply chain management, and many more. As such, it is essential for businesses and organizations to understand the potential of blockchain technology in ensuring the integrity of data processing and transfers, and to adopt this innovative technology to stay competitive and secure in the digital age.

Transparency and Auditability

Transparency and auditability are two essential components of any system that handles sensitive information. In recent years, blockchain technology has gained popularity due to its transparent and decentralized nature, which makes it an ideal solution for systems that require transparency and auditability.

In this chapter, we will explore how blockchain technology provides transparency and auditability, its benefits, and how it can be used to enhance accountability in various industries.

Transparency in Blockchain

Transparency is a critical component of blockchain technology. It refers to the ability to view and track all transactions and activities on the network. In a blockchain system, all transactions are recorded on a distributed ledger that is accessible to all network participants. This means that every transaction that occurs on the network can be tracked and verified by anyone on the network.

The transparency of blockchain technology has several benefits. For one, it provides a high level of accountability since every transaction is recorded and can be traced back to its source. This helps prevent fraud and ensures that transactions are conducted in a fair and transparent manner. Additionally, it can help build trust between network participants, as they can be confident that all transactions are being conducted honestly and accurately.

Auditability in Blockchain

Auditability is another important aspect of blockchain technology. It refers to the ability to verify and audit transactions and activities on the network. In a blockchain system, all transactions are verified by network participants, who use complex algorithms to validate transactions and add them to the distributed ledger.

The auditability of blockchain technology has several benefits. For one, it ensures that all transactions are accurate and secure, as they are verified by multiple network participants. This helps prevent fraud and ensures that all transactions are conducted in a trustworthy and reliable manner.

Blockchain technology also enables real-time auditing, which means that transactions can be audited and verified in real-time. This is particularly useful in industries that require frequent auditing, such as finance and healthcare.

Benefits of Transparency and Auditability in Blockchain

Transparency and auditability have several benefits in blockchain technology. One of the main advantages is that it enhances accountability and trust between network participants. When all transactions are recorded and verified on the network, it creates a sense of transparency and trust that can help build stronger relationships between network participants.

Transparency and auditability can also help prevent fraud and corruption, as all transactions are recorded and can be audited at any time. This can help reduce the risk of financial losses and ensure that all transactions are conducted in a fair and transparent manner.

Another advantage of transparency and auditability in blockchain technology is that it can improve compliance with regulations. Many industries are subject to strict regulations, and blockchain technology can help ensure that all transactions and activities are conducted in accordance with these regulations. The ability to audit transactions in real-time can help prevent violations and reduce the risk of penalties and fines.

Examples of Transparency and Auditability in Blockchain

Blockchain technology is being used in various industries to provide transparency and auditability. One of the most well-known examples is Bitcoin, which is a decentralized digital currency that operates on a blockchain network. All Bitcoin transactions are recorded on the blockchain, which provides a high level of transparency and auditability.

In the healthcare industry, blockchain technology is being used to enhance transparency and auditability. For example, blockchain can be used to track the supply chain of pharmaceuticals, ensuring that they are not counterfeit and are transported in a secure and transparent manner. Additionally, blockchain can be used to store patient records, providing a high level of security and privacy while still ensuring that records are auditable and transparent.

In the finance industry, blockchain technology is being used to enhance transparency and auditability. For example, blockchain can be used to track and verify stock trades, ensuring that they are conducted in a fair and transparent manner. Additionally, blockchain can be used to store financial records, providing a high level of transparency and auditability.

The use of blockchain technology in the finance industry can help prevent fraud, increase accountability, and improve regulatory compliance. With blockchain, all transactions are recorded on a transparent and immutable ledger, making it easier to track and verify financial transactions. This can help reduce the risk of fraud and increase transparency in the financial system.

Another area where blockchain technology can enhance transparency and auditability is supply chain management. With blockchain, businesses can track the movement of goods from their point of origin to their destination, ensuring that they are delivered in a timely and transparent manner. This can help reduce the risk of fraud, theft, and counterfeiting, and provide customers with greater confidence in the products they purchase.

In the healthcare industry, blockchain technology can also improve transparency and auditability. For example, blockchain can be used to track the movement of pharmaceuticals from the manufacturer to the end-user, ensuring that they are handled properly and not subject to tampering. Additionally, blockchain can be used to store patient records, providing a secure and transparent method of accessing and sharing medical data.

One of the key benefits of blockchain technology is that it provides a transparent and auditable record of all transactions. This makes it easier to identify and track fraudulent activities, reducing the risk of financial crimes and improving regulatory compliance. With blockchain, businesses can ensure that all transactions are conducted in a transparent and fair manner, enhancing the trust and confidence of their customers.

Furthermore, blockchain technology enables real-time tracking and monitoring of transactions, allowing businesses to identify and respond to potential issues quickly. This can help prevent the escalation of problems and reduce the impact on customers and stakeholders.

In conclusion, blockchain technology offers significant benefits in terms of transparency and auditability. Its decentralized and immutable nature provides a secure and transparent method of recording and tracking transactions, reducing the risk of fraud and enhancing regulatory compliance. By leveraging blockchain technology, businesses can improve transparency and accountability in a wide range of industries, from finance to healthcare to supply chain management. As blockchain technology continues to evolve, it is likely that we will see even more innovative uses and applications in the future.

Faster Transactions

How Blockchain Technology is Revolutionizing Payment Systems

In today's fast-paced world, speed is of the essence. This is particularly true when it comes to payment systems. Slow payment processing can lead to delays, frustration, and lost business opportunities. However, traditional payment systems are often slow and inefficient, with transactions taking days to complete. This is where blockchain technology comes in, offering a faster and more efficient way to process payments.

Blockchain technology can be used to create decentralized payment systems, enabling direct and immediate transfer of funds between parties. This eliminates the need for intermediaries such as banks and payment processors, which can slow down the payment process and increase costs.

The use of blockchain technology in payment systems offers several benefits, including faster transactions, lower costs, and increased security. In this chapter, we will explore how blockchain technology is revolutionizing payment systems and the benefits it offers.

Faster Transactions

One of the main benefits of blockchain technology in payment systems is the speed of transactions. Traditional payment systems often involve several intermediaries, which can slow down the payment process. With blockchain technology, payments can be made directly between parties, eliminating the need for intermediaries and reducing the time it takes to complete a transaction.

Blockchain technology enables real-time settlement of transactions, which means that funds can be transferred immediately. This is particularly useful for businesses that rely on quick payments, such as e-commerce retailers and service providers. With blockchain technology, these businesses can receive payment immediately, allowing them to process orders and provide services faster.

Lower Costs

Another benefit of using blockchain technology in payment systems is the reduction in costs. Traditional payment systems often involve several intermediaries, each of which charges a fee for their services. These fees can add up, increasing the overall cost of the payment process.

With blockchain technology, the need for intermediaries is eliminated, which reduces the fees associated with payment processing. This can lead to significant cost savings, particularly for businesses that process a large number of payments.

Increased Security

Security is a major concern when it comes to payment systems. Traditional payment systems are vulnerable to fraud, hacking, and other security breaches. Blockchain technology offers a more secure payment system by using cryptography and decentralized networks to ensure the security of transactions.

In a blockchain network, each transaction is verified by multiple nodes on the network, making it nearly impossible to tamper with. Additionally, blockchain technology uses cryptography to ensure the confidentiality and privacy of transactions.

Blockchain technology also eliminates the risk of chargebacks, which can occur in traditional payment systems. Chargebacks occur when a payment is disputed by the customer, and the funds are reversed. This can be costly for businesses, particularly those that process a high volume of transactions. With blockchain technology, transactions are irreversible, eliminating the risk of chargebacks.

Conclusion

Blockchain technology is revolutionizing payment systems, offering faster transactions, lower costs, and increased security. The use of blockchain technology in payment systems has the potential to transform the way we make and receive payments, making it more efficient and secure.

The benefits of blockchain technology in payment systems are particularly significant for businesses that rely on quick payments and low transaction costs. With blockchain technology, these businesses can process orders faster, reduce costs, and increase security.

As blockchain technology continues to evolve, we can expect to see even more benefits and use cases in payment systems. From micropayments to cross-border payments, blockchain technology has the potential to transform the way we conduct transactions, making it faster, more secure, and more efficient.

Lower Transaction Costs

Blockchain technology has revolutionized the way transactions are conducted, offering a secure, decentralized, and cost-effective alternative to traditional transaction methods. One of the most significant benefits of blockchain technology is the potential for lower transaction costs.

Traditional transaction methods, such as wire transfers or credit card transactions, often involve numerous intermediaries, such as banks, payment processors, and other financial institutions. Each of these intermediaries charges a fee for their services, resulting in high transaction costs for consumers and businesses.

In contrast, blockchain technology eliminates the need for intermediaries, allowing users to conduct transactions directly with one another. This direct transaction model reduces the number of intermediaries involved in a transaction, resulting in lower transaction costs.

Moreover, blockchain technology eliminates the need for many of the administrative costs associated with traditional transaction methods. For example, banks and other financial institutions must comply with various regulatory requirements, such as anti-money laundering (AML) and know your customer (KYC) regulations. These compliance costs are often passed on to consumers in the form of higher transaction fees.

With blockchain technology, compliance costs are significantly reduced because transactions are conducted on a decentralized network, and users can remain anonymous if desired. This reduction in compliance costs can result in lower transaction fees, making blockchain technology an attractive alternative for consumers and businesses.

Another factor contributing to lower transaction costs in blockchain technology is the use of smart contracts. Smart contracts are self-executing contracts with the terms of the agreement between buyer and seller being directly written into lines of code. Smart contracts eliminate the need for intermediaries, such as lawyers, and reduce the costs associated with drafting and executing traditional contracts.

Smart contracts can also reduce the transaction fees associated with third-party platforms, such as online marketplaces or e-commerce websites. For example, online marketplaces such as eBay charge transaction fees to both buyers and sellers for each transaction conducted on their platform. With blockchain technology and the use of smart contracts, the need for such platforms is eliminated, resulting in lower transaction fees.

The benefits of lower transaction costs in blockchain technology extend beyond financial transactions. For example, in supply chain management, blockchain technology can reduce the transaction costs associated with logistics and shipping. By enabling real-time tracking of products and services, blockchain technology can streamline the supply chain process, reduce the need for intermediaries, and lower transaction costs.

Additionally, in the healthcare industry, blockchain technology can help reduce the transaction costs associated with medical records. Currently, medical records are often stored in centralized databases, which can be expensive to maintain and can result in high transaction costs for patients and healthcare providers. By using blockchain technology, medical records can be securely stored on a decentralized network, reducing administrative costs and lowering transaction fees.

In conclusion, lower transaction costs are one of the most significant benefits of blockchain technology. By eliminating intermediaries and administrative costs, blockchain technology can significantly reduce transaction fees for consumers and businesses alike. With the use of smart contracts, blockchain technology can further reduce transaction costs and streamline the transaction process. As blockchain technology continues to evolve and gain widespread adoption, the potential for even lower transaction costs will continue to grow, making blockchain technology an increasingly attractive alternative to traditional transaction methods.

CHAPTER 15 - RISKS AND CHALLENGES OF BLOCKCHAIN TECHNOLOGY

Major Hurdles of Blockchain
Risks of Blockchain Technology
Legal and Regulatory Issues
Security Risks
Governance and Adoption Challenges

Chapter 15 delves into the various challenges and obstacles that have hindered the widespread adoption of blockchain technology. While the technology has immense potential to revolutionize industries, from finance to supply chain management, its adoption has been slow and uneven. In this chapter, we will explore some of the key factors that have contributed to this slow adoption, including issues with governance, scalability, and regulatory compliance. We will also discuss potential solutions to these challenges, as well as the future outlook for blockchain adoption.

Major Hurdles of Blockchain

Blockchain technology has been around for over a decade now and has seen widespread adoption in various industries. However, despite its potential and the benefits it offers, blockchain technology still faces several major hurdles that need to be overcome to reach its full potential. In this chapter, we will explore some of the major hurdles of blockchain technology.

Scalability

One of the major hurdles of blockchain technology is scalability. As more and more users join the network, the blockchain can become slower and less efficient in processing transactions. This is because every node in the network needs to verify each transaction, which can lead to a bottleneck in the system. Blockchain scalability is a complex problem that requires a combination of technological and economic solutions.

Several solutions have been proposed to address scalability, such as sharding, sidechains, and off-chain transactions. Sharding is a technique that involves breaking the blockchain into smaller pieces called shards, with each shard processing a subset of transactions. Sidechains are separate blockchains that are connected to the main blockchain, allowing for the processing of transactions off-chain. Off-chain transactions involve moving transactions off the blockchain to a separate network, reducing the load on the main blockchain.

Interoperability

Interoperability is another major hurdle of blockchain technology. Currently, there are several different blockchain platforms, each with its own set of standards and protocols. This can make it difficult for different blockchain platforms to communicate and work together, leading to silos of data and limited functionality.

To address interoperability, several initiatives have been launched, such as the Interledger Protocol and the Hyperledger Project. The Interledger Protocol is a protocol that allows different blockchain networks to communicate with each other, enabling the seamless transfer of value across different blockchains. The Hyperledger Project is an open-source project that aims to create a set of standards and protocols that can be used across different blockchain platforms.

Regulation

Regulation is another major hurdle of blockchain technology. The decentralized nature of blockchain technology makes it difficult for regulatory bodies to monitor and control the activities that take place on the blockchain. This can lead to concerns around money laundering, terrorist financing, and other illicit activities.

To address regulatory concerns, several initiatives have been launched, such as the Financial Action Task Force's guidelines on virtual assets and the European Union's proposed regulation of crypto assets. These initiatives aim to provide a framework for the regulation of blockchain technology and ensure that it is used in a responsible and ethical manner.

Security

Security is another major hurdle of blockchain technology. While blockchain technology is considered to be secure, it is not immune to attacks. For example, a 51% attack can occur when a single entity controls more than 50% of the mining power on a blockchain network, allowing them to manipulate the network and control the validation of transactions.

To address security concerns, several initiatives have been launched, such as the use of advanced cryptography and the development of consensus mechanisms that are resistant to attacks. Additionally, several blockchain platforms have implemented measures such as multi-factor authentication and cold storage of private keys to enhance security.

In conclusion, while blockchain technology has seen widespread adoption and has the potential to revolutionize many industries, it still faces several major hurdles that need to be overcome. Scalability, interoperability, regulation, and security are just some of the major challenges that need to be addressed to ensure that blockchain technology reaches its full potential. With continued research and development, it is hoped that these challenges can be overcome, paving the way for a more decentralized and secure future.

Risks of Blockchain Technology

Blockchain technology has gained significant attention in recent years due to its potential to revolutionize various industries. However, with its benefits come risks that need to be carefully considered and addressed. In this chapter, we will explore the risks of blockchain technology.

Security Risks

One of the most significant risks associated with blockchain technology is security. Blockchain networks are not entirely immune to attacks, and there have been several instances of successful attacks on blockchain networks, leading to loss of funds and personal information. One of the most prominent examples of a security breach in blockchain technology was the 2014 hack of Mt. Gox, which resulted in the loss of approximately 850,000 bitcoins, valued at over $450 million at the time.

Blockchain networks are secured through cryptography, but this does not guarantee complete security. The security of a blockchain network depends on several factors, including the design of the network, the consensus algorithm used, the level of decentralization, and the vulnerability of individual nodes. Therefore, it is crucial to implement robust security measures to protect blockchain networks from attacks.

Regulatory Risks

Blockchain technology operates in a largely unregulated environment, which can pose risks for both users and businesses. Governments around the world are grappling with how to regulate blockchain technology, with some countries adopting a more permissive approach while others are imposing strict regulations.

The lack of clear regulations around blockchain technology can create legal uncertainty, making it challenging for businesses to operate in the space. Additionally, regulatory risks can also impact the adoption of blockchain technology in regulated industries such as finance and healthcare.

Interoperability Risks

Interoperability refers to the ability of different blockchain networks to communicate and work together seamlessly. Currently, there is no standard for blockchain interoperability, which means that different blockchain networks operate independently of each other.

The lack of interoperability between blockchain networks can limit the potential of blockchain technology to transform industries. For example, in the healthcare industry, different healthcare providers may use different blockchain networks, making it challenging to share medical records between providers.

Scalability Risks

Scalability is a significant challenge for blockchain technology. As more users join a blockchain network, the network becomes slower and more expensive to use. This is because every node on the network must process every transaction, which can create bottlenecks and slow down the network.

To address scalability challenges, some blockchain networks have implemented solutions such as sharding and off-chain transactions. However, these solutions are not without their risks, and implementing them can be challenging.

Energy Consumption Risks

Proof of work consensus algorithms, which are used by many blockchain networks, require significant amounts of energy to operate. The energy consumption associated with proof of work is a significant concern, as it contributes to carbon emissions and climate change.

To address this issue, some blockchain networks have adopted alternative consensus algorithms such as proof of stake, which consume significantly less energy. However, these alternative consensus algorithms have their own challenges, such as the potential for centralization.

Conclusion

Blockchain technology has the potential to transform various industries, but it is not without its risks. Security, regulatory, interoperability, scalability, and energy consumption risks are significant challenges that must be carefully considered and addressed to ensure the widespread adoption and success of blockchain technology. Addressing these risks will require collaboration between stakeholders, including governments, businesses, and the blockchain community, to create a robust and secure blockchain ecosystem.

Legal and Regulatory Issues

Legal and regulatory issues are among the key challenges facing the widespread adoption of blockchain technology. As blockchain continues to evolve and grow, governments and regulatory bodies around the world are grappling with how to best regulate this new and disruptive technology.

One of the main concerns for regulators is how to ensure that blockchain technology is used for legal and ethical purposes. The decentralized and pseudonymous nature of blockchain has made it an attractive tool for illicit activities, such as money laundering and terrorism financing. Regulators are therefore tasked with striking a balance between supporting innovation while also protecting consumers and ensuring compliance with existing regulations.

Another challenge is the lack of harmonized regulatory frameworks across different jurisdictions. Blockchain technology is global, and as such, different countries and regions have varying legal and regulatory frameworks. This can lead to confusion and uncertainty for blockchain companies, which may have to navigate different regulations in different markets.

Moreover, blockchain technology poses new challenges for traditional legal frameworks. For example, smart contracts, which are self-executing agreements written in code on the blockchain, raise questions about contract law and the enforceability of such contracts. The concept of ownership of digital assets and how they are defined under existing laws is also a significant legal challenge. The immutability and irreversibility of transactions on the blockchain raise questions about property rights and how disputes can be resolved in the event of fraudulent or mistaken transactions.

Another significant legal challenge is data privacy and protection. While blockchain technology is inherently secure and transparent, it can also be challenging to ensure data privacy and protection in certain use cases. For example, in healthcare, blockchain technology can be used to securely store patient data, but there are concerns about how to ensure patient privacy while still allowing for the sharing of data between different healthcare providers.

Additionally, blockchain technology is still in its early stages of development, and legal and regulatory frameworks are still catching up. As such, there may be unforeseen legal and regulatory challenges that arise as the technology continues to evolve.

In conclusion, legal and regulatory issues are significant hurdles facing the widespread adoption of blockchain technology. While blockchain has the potential to revolutionize various industries, it is important that regulators strike a balance between innovation and protecting consumers while ensuring compliance with existing laws and regulations. Harmonized regulatory frameworks and clear guidelines for the use of blockchain technology can help mitigate legal and regulatory challenges, while continued innovation and collaboration between regulators and industry players can ensure that blockchain technology is used for legal and ethical purposes.

Security Risks

Security Risks of Blockchain Technology

Blockchain technology has been hailed as a breakthrough in secure and decentralized data management. Its inherent features such as immutability, decentralization, and transparency have made it attractive to businesses and governments looking to improve the security and integrity of their data. However, like any emerging technology, blockchain also poses several security risks that must be addressed to ensure the continued growth and adoption of the technology.

In this chapter, we will explore some of the significant security risks associated with blockchain technology and how they can be mitigated.

51% Attacks

A 51% attack, also known as a majority attack, is a type of security threat that can occur in blockchain networks that use a proof-of-work (PoW) consensus algorithm. In this attack, an attacker gains control of more than 51% of the network's computing power, enabling them to control the validation of new transactions and effectively disrupt the network's operation.

To carry out a 51% attack, the attacker must first acquire a significant amount of computing power, also known as a hash rate. Once they have control of the network, they can create and validate fraudulent transactions, effectively double-spending cryptocurrency. This type of attack can result in a significant loss of funds for the network's users and erode trust in the technology.

To mitigate the risk of 51% attacks, blockchain networks can implement a range of measures, such as increasing the number of nodes in the network, using a different consensus algorithm such as proof-of-stake (PoS), or implementing additional security measures such as multi-factor authentication for network participants.

Smart Contract Vulnerabilities

Smart contracts are self-executing computer programs that are stored on a blockchain network. They are designed to automate the execution of contracts and other legal agreements, making them an integral part of many blockchain-based applications.

However, smart contracts are susceptible to several security vulnerabilities that can be exploited by attackers. For example, programming errors can lead to bugs or loopholes in the code that can be exploited to steal or manipulate funds. Additionally, attackers can use social engineering tactics to trick users into executing malicious smart contracts.

To address smart contract vulnerabilities, blockchain developers can implement rigorous testing procedures and adopt best practices such as code reviews, automated testing, and third-party audits. Additionally, users should be cautious when interacting with smart contracts and only execute code from trusted sources.

Private Key Security

In blockchain networks, users hold private keys that are used to sign transactions and authorize the transfer of funds. These private keys are essential to the security of the network, as they provide a way for users to prove ownership of their cryptocurrency holdings.

However, private keys are susceptible to several security risks, such as theft, loss, or compromise. If a private key is lost or stolen, the user can lose access to their funds permanently. Additionally, if a private key falls into the wrong hands, an attacker can gain access to the user's cryptocurrency holdings and steal them.

To mitigate the risk of private key theft or loss, blockchain users should adopt best practices such as using hardware wallets, multi-signature wallets, and regularly backing up their private keys to secure storage. Additionally, blockchain networks can implement additional security measures such as two-factor authentication or multi-factor authentication to enhance the security of private keys.

Malware and Phishing Attacks

Malware and phishing attacks are common security risks associated with blockchain technology. Malware can be used to steal private keys or other sensitive data, while phishing attacks can be used to trick users into revealing their private keys or other sensitive information.

To mitigate the risk of malware and phishing attacks, blockchain users should adopt best practices such as using anti-virus software, regularly updating their software, and avoiding clicking on suspicious links or downloading unknown software. It is also recommended to use hardware wallets, which provide an additional layer of security by storing private keys offline.

Another security risk associated with blockchain technology is the potential for 51% attacks. In a blockchain network, consensus is reached through the agreement of a majority of nodes. A 51% attack occurs when a single entity or group of entities control more than 51% of the computing power on the network, giving them the ability to manipulate transactions and potentially double-spend coins.

While 51% attacks are difficult to carry out on large and well-established blockchain networks, smaller and newer networks may be more vulnerable. To mitigate this risk, blockchain networks often employ measures such as proof of stake or delegated proof of stake, which require users to hold a stake in the network and act as validators to prevent malicious actors from gaining control.

Finally, smart contract vulnerabilities pose a significant security risk in blockchain technology. Smart contracts are self-executing contracts that can be used to automate the execution of certain tasks, such as the transfer of assets. However, if a smart contract is not written properly, it can be vulnerable to exploitation by hackers, resulting in the loss of funds or other assets.

To mitigate the risk of smart contract vulnerabilities, blockchain developers should undergo thorough code audits and testing to identify and fix potential vulnerabilities. Additionally, users should exercise caution when using smart contracts and only use contracts that have been audited and verified by reputable third-party firms.

In conclusion, while blockchain technology provides numerous benefits, it also presents significant security risks. Malware and phishing attacks, 51% attacks, and smart contract vulnerabilities are just a few examples of the risks associated with blockchain technology. However, by implementing best practices and employing measures such as proof of stake and smart contract auditing, these risks can be mitigated, allowing for the continued growth and development of the blockchain ecosystem.

Governance and Adoption Challenge

Blockchain technology is still in its early stages, and as it continues to grow and develop, one of the key challenges it faces is governance and adoption. While blockchain technology offers numerous benefits, including increased security, transparency, and efficiency, it also presents a number of challenges that must be addressed to ensure its widespread adoption.

One of the biggest challenges facing blockchain technology is governance. Unlike traditional systems, blockchain technology is decentralized, meaning that no single entity has control over the network. This presents challenges in terms of decision-making and ensuring that the network operates in a fair and transparent manner.

Another challenge is the issue of scalability. Blockchain networks are currently limited in terms of the number of transactions they can process per second. As the number of users and transactions on the network grows, this can lead to slow transaction times and higher fees, making the network less appealing to users.

Regulatory challenges are also a major hurdle for blockchain technology. Due to its decentralized and anonymous nature, blockchain technology is often associated with illicit activities such as money laundering and drug trafficking. This has led to increased scrutiny from regulators, who are struggling to develop a framework for regulating blockchain technology that balances the need for security and transparency with the need to prevent illegal activities.

Another challenge facing blockchain technology is adoption. While there is a growing interest in blockchain technology, particularly in the financial industry, widespread adoption has been slow. This is due in part to a lack of awareness and understanding of the technology, as well as the challenges associated with implementing and integrating blockchain into existing systems.

To address these challenges, a number of solutions are being developed. In terms of governance, various models are being explored, including on-chain and off-chain governance models. On-chain governance allows for decisions to be made directly on the blockchain, while off-chain governance involves using separate mechanisms to make decisions about the network.

Scalability is also being addressed through the development of new protocols and technologies, such as sharding and sidechains. Sharding involves breaking up the blockchain into smaller, more manageable pieces, while sidechains allow for transactions to be processed outside of the main blockchain, improving speed and efficiency.

Regulatory challenges are being addressed through the development of regulatory frameworks and guidelines, as well as the use of tools such as Know Your Customer (KYC) and Anti-Money Laundering (AML) policies to prevent illicit activities on the blockchain.

Finally, to encourage adoption, efforts are being made to increase awareness and understanding of blockchain technology, as well as to make it easier to integrate into existing systems. This includes the development of user-friendly interfaces, as well as the use of APIs and other tools to simplify integration.

In conclusion, while blockchain technology offers numerous benefits, it also presents a number of challenges that must be addressed to ensure its widespread adoption. Governance, scalability, regulatory issues, and adoption are just a few of the challenges that must be overcome to fully realize the potential of blockchain technology. However, with continued innovation and collaboration, these challenges can be addressed, and blockchain technology can become a key component of the digital economy.

CHAPTER 16 - DECIDING IF BLOCKCHAIN TECHNOLOGY IS RIGHT FOR YOU

- ❖ Who Will Be Looking at Your Data?
- ❖ Writable Data
- ❖ Data Alteration
- ❖ Data Restoration
- ❖ Easy to Share
- ❖ Storage Limitations
- ❖ Verification Process
- ❖ Taking the Next Step

Who Will Be Looking at Your Data?

In today's digital age, data is a valuable asset, and its collection and use have become essential for many businesses and organizations. However, with the increasing amount of personal information being collected, concerns about data privacy and security have risen. In particular, the question of who has access to your data has become a significant concern for many individuals.

In the past, individuals had a better understanding of who had access to their data. They could control who they shared their information with and had a good idea of who was collecting their data. However, with the rise of the internet and the use of digital technologies, the collection and sharing of personal data have become much more complex. Many individuals are now unsure of who has access to their data and how it is being used.

This chapter will explore the issue of who has access to your data and how it is being used. We will discuss the various ways in which data is collected, stored, and shared, and the implications of this for individual privacy and security. We will also look at some of the steps that individuals can take to protect their data and ensure that only authorized parties have access to it.

Data Collection and Sharing

One of the primary ways in which personal data is collected is through online platforms and services. Social media platforms, search engines, and e-commerce websites all collect and store data about their users. This data is used to personalize user experiences, provide targeted advertising, and improve the overall functionality of the platform or service.

Many individuals are unaware of the extent to which their data is being collected and shared. For example, social media platforms often collect information about users' location, browsing history, and even the content of their private messages. This data can be used to build a detailed profile of the individual and can be shared with third-party advertisers or other organizations.

Data Breaches

Another issue related to data privacy and security is the risk of data breaches. Data breaches occur when sensitive information is accessed or stolen by unauthorized parties. This can result in the exposure of personal information, such as credit card numbers, social security numbers, and other sensitive data.

Data breaches can occur in a variety of ways, including through hacking, malware, and phishing attacks. In many cases, these breaches are the result of poor security practices by organizations that collect and store personal data.

Implications for Privacy and Security

The collection and sharing of personal data have significant implications for individual privacy and security. For example, the data collected by online platforms can be used to create targeted advertising, which can be seen as a violation of privacy. Additionally, the exposure of personal data through data breaches can lead to identity theft, financial fraud, and other serious consequences.

In some cases, the sharing of personal data can also result in discrimination. For example, insurance companies may use data about an individual's health or lifestyle to deny coverage or charge higher premiums. Similarly, employers may use data about an individual's social media activity to make hiring decisions.

Protecting Your Data

Given the potential risks associated with the collection and sharing of personal data, it is important for individuals to take steps to protect their data. Some of the steps that individuals can take include:

Being aware of what data is being collected and how it is being used.

Using strong passwords and two-factor authentication to secure online accounts.

Regularly updating software and anti-virus programs to protect against malware and other threats.

Being cautious when sharing personal information online, especially on social media platforms.

Being aware of the privacy settings on online platforms and adjusting them as needed.

Conclusion

The issue of who has access to your data and how it is being used is a complex one that requires careful consideration. As data collection and sharing become more prevalent, it is important for individuals to be aware of the risks and take steps to protect their personal information.

While blockchain technology can offer some solutions to the issue of data privacy, it is not a one-size-fits-all solution. The decentralized nature of blockchain can provide individuals with more control over their data and allow for transparency in its use, but it also brings new challenges such as the potential for data breaches and the need for consensus among network participants.

As blockchain technology continues to evolve, it will be essential for individuals and organizations to develop robust data governance policies and strategies. This includes implementing effective security measures, providing transparency and accountability in data use, and ensuring compliance with legal and regulatory requirements.

In addition, individuals can take steps to protect their personal data by being cautious about the information they share online and using privacy-enhancing technologies such as virtual private networks (VPNs) and encryption.

Overall, the issue of data privacy is a complex and ongoing challenge that requires collaboration and ongoing efforts to address. While blockchain technology offers some potential solutions, it is only one piece of the puzzle, and a comprehensive approach to data privacy is necessary to protect individuals and their sensitive information.

Writable Data

Writable data refers to information that can be edited or updated by authorized parties. In the context of technology and data management, writable data is crucial as it enables changes to be made to data sets, making them more accurate and up-to-date. While this may seem like a positive aspect, there are also potential risks and challenges associated with writable data.

One of the primary benefits of writable data is the ability to update and correct inaccuracies in real-time. This is particularly important in industries such as healthcare, where patient records need to be updated quickly and accurately. With writable data, authorized personnel can make changes to patient records as soon as they become available, ensuring that the records are always current and accurate.

Another benefit of writable data is its versatility. Writable data can be used to store a variety of information types, including text, images, and video. This flexibility makes it an ideal tool for storing and managing large amounts of data.

However, with the ability to edit and update data also comes the risk of unauthorized changes. Malicious actors can manipulate writable data for personal gain or to cause harm. This is particularly concerning in industries such as finance, where the integrity of data is critical. A single unauthorized change could have severe consequences and lead to financial losses.

To mitigate the risks associated with writable data, it is important to implement robust security measures. This includes implementing access controls to ensure that only authorized personnel can make changes to data sets. Additionally, regular audits and monitoring can help detect any unauthorized changes.

One challenge associated with writable data is ensuring the accuracy and consistency of changes made to data sets. With multiple parties potentially making changes, there is a risk of conflicting updates or incomplete changes. This can lead to data inconsistencies and errors, making it challenging to use the data effectively.

To address this challenge, it is important to establish clear data management protocols that outline who is responsible for making changes and how they should be made. Additionally, implementing version control systems can help track changes and ensure that all updates are properly documented.

Another challenge associated with writable data is the potential for data loss. This can occur if changes are made without proper backups or if the data is not stored securely. In industries such as healthcare or finance, the loss of data can have severe consequences and lead to legal and financial liabilities.

To mitigate the risk of data loss, it is important to establish robust backup and recovery systems. This includes regularly backing up data to secure offsite locations and implementing disaster recovery protocols.

In conclusion, while writable data provides many benefits, it also presents potential risks and challenges. To ensure that writable data is effectively managed and secured, it is important to implement robust security measures, establish clear data management protocols, and regularly monitor and audit data sets. With these measures in place, organizations can leverage the benefits of writable data while mitigating potential risks.

Data Alteration

In today's digital age, data is becoming increasingly important, and the ability to trust the accuracy and authenticity of that data is crucial. Blockchain technology has emerged as a promising solution for ensuring data integrity and immutability, as it provides a tamper-proof and decentralized platform for recording and storing data. However, even with the security features provided by blockchain technology, data alteration remains a significant risk that must be addressed.

Data alteration refers to the unauthorized modification or manipulation of data by an attacker. This can take many forms, such as changing the content of a message, altering financial records, or modifying sensitive personal information. The impact of data alteration can be severe, ranging from financial losses and reputational damage to identity theft and national security threats.

Blockchain technology offers several features that make it difficult to alter data stored on the blockchain. These include immutability, transparency, and decentralized consensus. However, there are still several ways in which data alteration can occur, and it is important to understand the risks and how to mitigate them.

Insider Threats

One of the most significant risks to data alteration on the blockchain comes from insider threats. These are individuals who have authorized access to the system and use their privileges to manipulate or alter data for personal gain or malicious intent. Insider threats can be difficult to detect, as they are often familiar with the system and its security measures.

To mitigate the risk of insider threats, it is essential to have a comprehensive security policy in place that includes access controls, monitoring, and auditing. Additionally, regular training and awareness programs can help employees understand the importance of data integrity and the consequences of altering data.

51% Attack

A 51% attack is a situation where an individual or group of individuals control more than 50% of the computing power on a blockchain network, enabling them to manipulate the data on the blockchain. This type of attack is typically seen in proof-of-work (PoW) blockchains, where computing power is used to validate transactions and create new blocks.

To mitigate the risk of a 51% attack, some blockchain networks use a consensus mechanism that requires a large number of nodes to agree on the validity of each block. This makes it difficult for any one entity to control the network and alter data.

Smart Contract Vulnerabilities
Smart contracts are self-executing contracts with the terms of the agreement written into code on the blockchain. While they are designed to be secure and tamper-proof, smart contracts are vulnerable to coding errors and vulnerabilities that can be exploited by attackers.

To mitigate the risk of smart contract vulnerabilities, it is important to conduct rigorous code reviews and security testing before deploying a smart contract. Additionally, regular audits and monitoring can help identify and address any vulnerabilities that are discovered.

External Data Sources

Blockchain technology can also be vulnerable to data alteration through external data sources. For example, if an oracle that provides external data to a smart contract is compromised, it could result in incorrect or manipulated data being used in the contract.

To mitigate the risk of external data sources, it is important to use trusted and verified sources of data. Additionally, it may be possible to use multiple data sources and consensus algorithms to verify the accuracy of the data.

Forks

A fork occurs when there is a disagreement among members of a blockchain network about the rules governing the network, resulting in the creation of a new blockchain that is separate from the original. Forks can occur for a variety of reasons, such as a change in the consensus mechanism or a disagreement over the validity of a transaction.

While forks are a legitimate part of the blockchain ecosystem, they can also be used as a means of data alteration. For example, an attacker could initiate a fork and manipulate the data on the new blockchain.

To mitigate the risk of data alteration through forks, blockchain networks must have clear governance structures in place to prevent unauthorized changes. This can include mechanisms for resolving disputes and establishing clear rules for network participants.

Another approach to reducing the risk of data alteration through forks is to increase the difficulty of forking. This can be achieved by implementing stricter consensus mechanisms or by increasing the number of nodes required to initiate a fork.

In addition to forks, there are other methods that can be used to alter data on a blockchain, such as 51% attacks and double-spending attacks.

A 51% attack occurs when an individual or group controls a majority of the computing power in a blockchain network, allowing them to manipulate the blockchain's transaction history. This type of attack is often used to carry out double-spending attacks, where an attacker spends the same cryptocurrency multiple times by manipulating the transaction history.

To prevent 51% attacks, blockchain networks can implement mechanisms such as proof-of-stake or proof-of-authority, which require participants to hold a certain amount of cryptocurrency or demonstrate their identity and reputation within the network.

Double-spending attacks can also be prevented through the use of consensus mechanisms and transaction verification processes. For example, in Bitcoin, each transaction must be verified by multiple nodes in the network before it is added to the blockchain, making it more difficult to carry out double-spending attacks.

Ultimately, the prevention of data alteration on a blockchain requires a combination of technical and governance measures. By implementing clear rules and governance structures, increasing the difficulty of forking and attacks, and utilizing strong consensus mechanisms and transaction verification processes, blockchain networks can maintain the integrity of their data and provide a secure foundation for decentralized applications and services.

Data Restoration

Data restoration refers to the process of recovering data that has been lost, damaged, or corrupted. In traditional centralized systems, data restoration is often a complex and time-consuming process, requiring a significant amount of resources and specialized expertise. However, blockchain technology offers a new approach to data restoration that is more efficient and reliable.

One of the key advantages of blockchain technology is its decentralized nature. Because there is no central authority controlling the network, data is stored on a distributed ledger that is replicated across all nodes in the network. This means that even if one node fails or becomes compromised, the data can still be retrieved from other nodes in the network.

In addition, blockchain technology uses cryptographic algorithms to ensure the integrity and security of the data. Each block in the blockchain is linked to the previous block in a chain, forming a tamper-evident record of all transactions. This makes it virtually impossible to alter or manipulate data on the blockchain without being detected.

These features make blockchain technology an ideal solution for data restoration in a variety of contexts. For example, in the healthcare industry, blockchain technology can be used to securely store and share patient data, which is often subject to loss or corruption due to the complex nature of healthcare systems.

Blockchain technology can also be used to restore data in the event of a cyber attack or other security breach. Because the data is distributed across multiple nodes, it is more difficult for attackers to gain access to the entire system and steal or alter the data. In the event of a successful attack, the decentralized nature of the blockchain makes it easier to identify the compromised nodes and restore the data from other nodes in the network.

Another application of blockchain technology for data restoration is in the area of disaster recovery. In the event of a natural disaster or other catastrophic event that causes data loss, blockchain technology can be used to quickly and efficiently restore the lost data. Because the data is distributed across multiple nodes, it is less vulnerable to loss or corruption than centralized data storage systems.

In order to take advantage of these benefits, organizations must adopt blockchain technology and develop strategies for integrating it into their existing data management systems. This may require significant investment in new infrastructure, as well as training and education for staff.

One of the key challenges of implementing blockchain technology for data restoration is the need to balance security with accessibility. While the decentralized nature of the blockchain makes it more secure, it also makes it more difficult to access and retrieve data. This can be particularly challenging in emergency situations where time is of the essence.

Another challenge is the need to ensure interoperability between different blockchain networks. As blockchain technology continues to evolve, there is a risk of fragmentation as different networks develop their own protocols and standards. This could make it difficult to restore data across different networks, particularly in cases where the data is sensitive or critical.

Despite these challenges, the potential benefits of blockchain technology for data restoration are significant. By providing a more secure and efficient method of restoring lost or damaged data, blockchain technology has the potential to revolutionize the way organizations manage their data and respond to crises.

Easy to Share

Data sharing has become an increasingly important aspect of our modern digital world. With the rise of big data, machine learning, and artificial intelligence, the ability to access and share vast amounts of information is critical for businesses, governments, and individuals alike. However, with data sharing come both benefits and risks. In this chapter, we will explore the advantages and drawbacks of data sharing, as well as the best practices for ensuring that data is shared safely and securely.

Advantages of Data Sharing

One of the primary benefits of data sharing is that it enables organizations and individuals to make more informed decisions. By accessing and analyzing large datasets, businesses can gain insights into market trends, consumer behavior, and other factors that can inform their strategies and improve their bottom line. Similarly, governments can use data to inform policy decisions, identify areas of need, and monitor public health.

Data sharing can also lead to more collaboration and innovation. When organizations and individuals share information, they can build on each other's work, find new solutions to complex problems, and make progress more quickly than they could working in isolation. For example, researchers in different parts of the world can collaborate on a medical study, sharing data and insights to develop new treatments or therapies.

Another advantage of data sharing is that it can help to promote transparency and accountability. When organizations are required to share their data with the public, it can help to ensure that they are operating ethically and legally. Similarly, when individuals are able to access their own data, they can ensure that it is accurate and up-to-date, and make decisions about how it is used.

Risks of Data Sharing

While data sharing can provide many benefits, it also comes with certain risks. One of the primary risks is the potential for data breaches and cyber attacks. When data is shared, it is more vulnerable to theft or unauthorized access. This can lead to a range of problems, from financial loss to identity theft to reputational damage.

Data sharing can also raise concerns about privacy. When individuals share their data, they may not fully understand how it will be used, or who will have access to it. This can be especially problematic when sensitive or personal information is involved, such as medical records or financial data.

Another risk of data sharing is that it can be used to discriminate against individuals or groups. For example, if an employer collects data on their employees' social media use, they may use this information to make decisions about hiring, firing, or promotions. This could lead to discrimination against individuals based on their race, gender, or other factors.

Best Practices for Safe and Secure Data Sharing

To ensure that data is shared safely and securely, it is important to follow best practices. Here are some tips for safe data sharing:

Use encryption: When sharing data, use encryption to protect it from unauthorized access. Encryption scrambles data so that it can only be read by someone with the proper key or password.

Limit access: Only share data with individuals or organizations that have a legitimate need to access it. This can help to reduce the risk of data breaches or unauthorized access.

Obtain consent: When sharing personal or sensitive data, obtain consent from the individual first. This can help to ensure that they understand how their data will be used, and can provide an opportunity for them to opt out if they choose.

Secure networks: When sharing data over a network, make sure that the network is secure and protected from cyber attacks.

Monitor use: Regularly monitor the use of shared data to ensure that it is being used in accordance with the agreed-upon terms. This can help to prevent misuse or abuse of the data.

Conclusion

Data sharing has become a critical aspect of our modern digital world, enabling organizations to collaborate, innovate and deliver better services. However, it also poses risks to data privacy and security, particularly when sensitive information is shared without proper protection or consent. Therefore, it is important to ensure that data sharing practices are done in a responsible and secure manner.

In this chapter, we have discussed the benefits and challenges of data sharing, as well as some best practices to ensure data security and privacy. Data sharing can lead to better decision-making, increased efficiency, and improved collaboration among stakeholders. However, it can also result in data breaches, misuse of personal information, and legal or regulatory non-compliance.

To mitigate these risks, organizations must implement robust data security and privacy measures, including access controls, data encryption, and data governance policies. They should also ensure that all stakeholders understand the importance of data privacy and security and are aware of their responsibilities.

Furthermore, organizations should consider adopting emerging technologies such as blockchain to enhance the security and transparency of data sharing. Blockchain provides a decentralized and immutable platform for data sharing, reducing the risk of unauthorized access, tampering, and fraud.

In conclusion, data sharing is a vital component of modern business operations and innovation, but it also poses significant risks to data privacy and security. Organizations must implement robust data security measures and educate all stakeholders on their responsibilities to ensure responsible and secure data sharing practices. Additionally, emerging technologies such as blockchain can provide additional security and transparency to data sharing, which can enhance trust among stakeholders and support innovation.

Storage Limitations

The amount of data being generated in our digital world is growing exponentially, and it has become increasingly challenging to store and manage this data efficiently. One of the most significant challenges in data storage is the limitation of physical storage devices.

Traditional storage devices, such as hard disk drives (HDDs) and solid-state drives (SSDs), have limited storage capacities. HDDs typically have a capacity of several terabytes, while SSDs have a capacity of up to several hundred gigabytes. While these capacities may seem large, they can quickly become insufficient when dealing with large amounts of data.

To address the limitations of traditional storage devices, many organizations have turned to cloud storage solutions. Cloud storage providers offer virtually unlimited storage capacities and can scale up or down to meet the needs of their customers. Additionally, cloud storage is often more cost-effective than traditional storage devices, as organizations only pay for the storage they use.

Despite the benefits of cloud storage, it also poses several challenges. One of the main concerns is data security. Storing data in the cloud means that the data is stored on servers outside of the organization's premises, making it more vulnerable to cyberattacks. Therefore, organizations must ensure that they implement adequate security measures, such as encryption and access control, to protect their data.

Another challenge with cloud storage is the potential for downtime or service outages. If a cloud storage provider experiences a service interruption, organizations may be unable to access their data, causing significant disruptions to their operations. To mitigate this risk, organizations should ensure that their cloud storage provider offers high availability and redundancy options to minimize the risk of downtime.

Another potential limitation of data storage is the physical lifespan of storage devices. All storage devices have a limited lifespan, and they will eventually fail, potentially leading to data loss. To mitigate this risk, organizations should implement backup and disaster recovery plans to ensure that their data is recoverable in the event of a storage device failure.

Additionally, as data storage capacities continue to grow, the need for more efficient and sustainable storage solutions becomes increasingly important. The energy consumption required to power and cool large data centers can be significant, contributing to environmental concerns. Therefore, organizations should consider using more energy-efficient storage solutions, such as solid-state drives and flash storage, and explore renewable energy options to power their data centers.

In conclusion, data storage limitations are a significant challenge for organizations in the digital age. Traditional storage devices have limited capacities, and cloud storage solutions pose security and downtime risks. Organizations must implement adequate security measures, backup and disaster recovery plans, and explore more sustainable storage options to ensure they can efficiently manage and store their data.

Verification Process

The verification process is an essential aspect of data management, ensuring that the data is accurate, trustworthy, and reliable. It involves the process of confirming the authenticity, accuracy, and completeness of the data. Verification is a critical step in the data management process, as it ensures that the data can be trusted for decision-making and other critical functions.

In traditional data management systems, verification is often done manually, which can be time-consuming and error-prone. However, with the advent of modern technologies such as blockchain and artificial intelligence, the verification process has become more automated and efficient.

Verification in Blockchain

Blockchain technology has revolutionized the verification process by providing a decentralized system that eliminates the need for intermediaries. In a blockchain network, transactions are verified and confirmed by a network of nodes, ensuring that the data is accurate and tamper-proof. The decentralized nature of the blockchain network ensures that there is no single point of failure, making it more secure and resilient.

One of the primary benefits of blockchain technology is its ability to create a trustless system. This means that the verification process does not require trust between parties, as the blockchain network itself is responsible for verifying the data. Each transaction on the blockchain network is verified by a network of nodes, with each node independently verifying the data to ensure its accuracy and authenticity. Once a transaction has been verified and confirmed, it is added to the blockchain, creating an immutable record that cannot be altered.

Verification with Artificial Intelligence

Artificial intelligence (AI) is another technology that is transforming the verification process. AI algorithms can analyze vast amounts of data and identify patterns and anomalies, making it easier to detect errors and inconsistencies in the data. AI-powered verification can help organizations to identify fraudulent activities and prevent data breaches, improving the overall accuracy and reliability of the data.

AI algorithms can also learn from historical data, improving their accuracy over time. This means that the more data that is analyzed, the more accurate the verification process becomes. As AI technology continues to develop, it is likely that it will become an increasingly important tool for data verification.

However, AI-based verification processes are not without their challenges. One major challenge is the potential for bias in the data used to train the algorithms. AI algorithms learn from historical data, and if that data is biased, it can lead to biased results. For example, if historical data shows a disproportionate number of loan applications from men are approved compared to women, an AI algorithm trained on that data may perpetuate that bias by automatically rejecting more loan applications from women.

To address this challenge, it is important to ensure that the data used to train AI algorithms is diverse and representative of the population. This can be achieved through careful selection of data sources and the use of diverse data sets.

Another challenge with AI-based verification is the potential for adversarial attacks. Adversarial attacks are techniques used to manipulate or trick AI algorithms into making incorrect decisions. For example, an attacker may modify an image in a way that is imperceptible to humans but causes an AI algorithm to misidentify the image. These attacks can be particularly concerning in applications such as facial recognition, where the consequences of a misidentification can be significant.

To address this challenge, researchers are developing algorithms that are more robust against adversarial attacks. One approach is to train AI algorithms on a combination of clean and adversarial examples, which can help them better recognize and defend against attacks.

Finally, there is the challenge of explainability. AI-based verification processes can be difficult to explain, as the algorithms used can be complex and opaque. This can be problematic in situations where decisions made by AI algorithms have significant consequences, such as in healthcare or financial services.

To address this challenge, researchers are developing methods for explaining how AI algorithms make decisions. One approach is to use so-called "explainable AI" techniques, which aim to provide insights into how algorithms arrived at their decisions. This can help to build trust in AI-based verification processes and ensure that decisions are fair and transparent.

In conclusion, AI has the potential to revolutionize the data verification process, making it faster, more accurate, and more efficient. However, as with any technology, there are challenges that must be addressed to ensure that AI-based verification is robust and reliable. By addressing issues such as bias, adversarial attacks, and explainability, we can develop AI-based verification systems that are fair, transparent, and trustworthy.

Taking the Next Step

As we have seen throughout this book, blockchain technology has the potential to revolutionize numerous industries, from finance to healthcare to supply chain management. However, the technology is still relatively new and there are many challenges that need to be overcome before it can reach its full potential. In this chapter, we will discuss some of the steps that can be taken to further the development and adoption of blockchain technology.

Collaboration and Standardization

One of the biggest obstacles to widespread adoption of blockchain technology is the lack of collaboration and standardization among different blockchain networks. There are currently numerous blockchain platforms, each with their own unique features and specifications. This fragmentation can make it difficult for developers and organizations to build on top of existing networks and can slow down the development of new blockchain applications.

To address this issue, there needs to be more collaboration and standardization within the blockchain community. This could involve the development of common protocols and standards that can be used across multiple blockchain networks. It could also involve greater collaboration between blockchain developers and industry experts to identify the most pressing needs and use cases for blockchain technology.

Education and Awareness

Another challenge facing the blockchain community is the lack of education and awareness about the technology. Many people still associate blockchain primarily with cryptocurrencies like Bitcoin, and are not aware of the broader potential applications of the technology.

To overcome this challenge, there needs to be greater education and awareness about the benefits of blockchain technology. This could involve targeted outreach efforts to specific industries and communities, as well as public education campaigns to raise awareness among the general public. It could also involve the development of educational resources, such as online courses and tutorials, to help individuals and organizations learn more about blockchain technology and how to use it effectively.

Regulatory Frameworks

Another challenge facing the adoption of blockchain technology is the lack of clear regulatory frameworks governing the use of the technology. As blockchain technology continues to be applied to a wider range of industries and use cases, there is a need for clear guidelines and regulations to ensure that the technology is being used in a safe and responsible manner.

To address this challenge, there needs to be greater collaboration between blockchain developers and policymakers to develop regulatory frameworks that are appropriate for the unique features and capabilities of blockchain technology. This could involve the establishment of regulatory sandboxes, where blockchain startups and developers can test new applications in a controlled environment. It could also involve the development of industry-led standards and guidelines that can be used to inform government regulations.

Scalability and Interoperability

One of the most significant technical challenges facing the blockchain community is scalability and interoperability. As more users and organizations adopt blockchain technology, there is a need for networks to be able to handle larger volumes of transactions and support interoperability between different blockchain networks.

To address this challenge, there needs to be greater investment in research and development focused on scalability and interoperability. This could involve the development of new consensus mechanisms and protocols that are better suited to handling larger volumes of transactions. It could also involve the development of cross-chain communication protocols that enable different blockchain networks to communicate with each other.

Continued Innovation

Finally, to realize the full potential of blockchain technology, there needs to be a continued focus on innovation and experimentation. Blockchain technology is still in its early stages of development, and there are likely many new applications and use cases that have yet to be discovered.

To foster innovation, there needs to be greater investment in blockchain research and development. This could involve the establishment of research institutions and academic programs focused on blockchain technology, as well as the development of innovation hubs and incubators to support blockchain startups and entrepreneurs.

Conclusion

Blockchain technology has the potential to transform the way we store, manage, and share data. However, there are many challenges that need to be overcome before the technology can reach its full potential.

CHAPTER 17 - BLOCKCHAIN IMPLEMENTATION MISTAKES TO AVOID

- ❖ Having Unrealistic Expectations
- ❖ Underestimating the Time Commitment
- ❖ Being Impatient
- ❖ Not Limiting Access: The Risks of Unrestricted Access to Blockchain Data
- ❖ Poor Planning
- ❖ Lack of Clear Objectives
- ❖ Failing to Build a Support Network

Blockchain technology has garnered a lot of attention and excitement in recent years, with many viewing it as a game-changer for various industries. While the potential of blockchain technology is undeniable, it is essential to approach it with a realistic mindset and an understanding of its limitations. Unrealistic expectations, impatience, poor planning, and a lack of clear objectives are some of the common mistakes that can hinder successful implementation of blockchain technology. In this chapter, we will explore one of these challenges: not limiting access.

Having Unrealistic Expectations

Blockchain technology has been hailed as a revolutionary technology that has the potential to transform many industries. Its decentralized, immutable, and transparent nature has led many to believe that it can solve a wide range of problems, from streamlining supply chains to revolutionizing finance. While blockchain technology does have the potential to create significant change, it is important to be aware of the limitations and potential pitfalls of the technology.

One of the most significant challenges associated with blockchain technology is having unrealistic expectations. This can lead to disappointment and a loss of faith in the technology when it fails to live up to its perceived potential. In this chapter, we will explore some of the unrealistic expectations that people have regarding blockchain technology.

Blockchain technology can solve all problems
One of the most common unrealistic expectations associated with blockchain technology is the belief that it can solve all problems. While blockchain technology does have the potential to create significant change, it is not a silver bullet that can solve every problem. Blockchain technology is not suitable for all applications, and in some cases, it may not be the most efficient or effective solution.

For example, while blockchain technology can be used to create a transparent and secure ledger, it may not be the best solution for storing large amounts of data. In addition, blockchain technology may not be suitable for applications that require high-speed transactions or real-time data processing.

Blockchain technology is completely secure
Another unrealistic expectation associated with blockchain technology is the belief that it is completely secure. While blockchain technology is inherently more secure than traditional centralized systems, it is not completely immune to security breaches. Hackers have already demonstrated that they can exploit vulnerabilities in blockchain systems to steal cryptocurrency or manipulate data.

In addition, blockchain technology is only as secure as the systems that interact with it. If a user's private key is compromised, an attacker can gain access to their blockchain account and steal their cryptocurrency or manipulate data.

Blockchain technology is easy to implement
Another common misconception about blockchain technology is that it is easy to implement. In reality, implementing blockchain technology can be a complex and time-consuming process that requires significant resources and expertise.

For example, organizations that want to implement blockchain technology must first determine which blockchain platform to use, such as Ethereum or Hyperledger. They must then develop smart contracts, which are self-executing contracts that are stored on the blockchain. Developing smart contracts requires expertise in blockchain development, as well as knowledge of programming languages such as Solidity.

Blockchain technology will replace all centralized systems
There is a belief among some enthusiasts that blockchain technology will eventually replace all centralized systems, such as banks and governments. While it is true that blockchain technology can disrupt centralized systems, it is unlikely that it will completely replace them.

Centralized systems have existed for centuries and serve an important role in our society. Blockchain technology can create new opportunities and improve efficiency, but it is unlikely to replace centralized systems entirely.

Blockchain technology is a get-rich-quick scheme
Finally, one of the most dangerous unrealistic expectations associated with blockchain technology is the belief that it is a get-rich-quick scheme. While it is true that some early adopters of blockchain technology have become wealthy, it is not a guaranteed path to riches.

Investing in blockchain technology carries significant risks, just like any other investment. The value of cryptocurrencies can be highly volatile and can fluctuate rapidly. In addition, investing in blockchain technology requires knowledge and expertise in the field, as well as an understanding of the risks associated with investing.

Conclusion:

Blockchain technology has the potential to create significant change in many industries, but it is important to be aware of the limitations and potential pitfalls of the technology. Having unrealistic expectations can lead to disappointment and a loss of faith in the technology when it fails to live up to its perceived potential. By understanding the limitations and challenges of blockchain, individuals and organizations can better manage their expectations and make more informed decisions about how to use the technology.

One key factor in managing expectations is to recognize that blockchain is not a cure-all solution for every problem. While it has the potential to create more transparent and secure systems, it may not be the best solution for every use case. It is important to carefully consider the specific needs and goals of a project before deciding whether or not to use blockchain technology.

Another factor to consider is the timeline for realizing the benefits of blockchain technology. While some early adopters of blockchain have seen impressive results, widespread adoption and integration of the technology may take years or even decades. It is important to be patient and recognize that change takes time.

Additionally, it is important to recognize that blockchain technology is still evolving and improving. New developments and advancements are being made regularly, and what may seem like a limitation or challenge today may be resolved in the future. It is important to stay informed about new developments and advancements in the technology in order to make the most of its potential.

Finally, it is important to remember that blockchain technology is not immune to human error or malfeasance. While it may be more secure and transparent than traditional systems, it is still vulnerable to hacking, insider threats, and other security risks. It is important to implement robust security measures and best practices to minimize these risks and protect sensitive data.

In conclusion, managing expectations is a crucial aspect of successfully leveraging the potential of blockchain technology. By recognizing its limitations and challenges, understanding the timeline for realizing benefits, staying informed about new developments and advancements, and implementing robust security measures, individuals and organizations can make more informed decisions about how to use blockchain technology and avoid disappointment and disillusionment.

Ultimately, blockchain technology has the potential to create significant positive change in many industries, but it is up to us to manage our expectations and use the technology responsibly and effectively.

Underestimating the Time Commitment

Blockchain technology has captured the imagination of many, and for good reason. It promises to revolutionize the way we conduct transactions, store data, and interact with each other. However, the road to widespread adoption is not without its challenges. One such challenge is the issue of impatience.

Impatience is a common issue when it comes to emerging technologies. People often expect immediate results, and when those results don't materialize, they may become disillusioned or lose faith in the technology altogether. This can be particularly damaging when it comes to blockchain technology, which is still in its early stages of development and implementation.

One of the main reasons for impatience is the hype that surrounds blockchain technology. Many people have heard about the potential of blockchain to disrupt industries, create new business models, and solve complex problems. However, what they may not realize is that this will not happen overnight. Blockchain is a complex technology that requires significant investment and expertise to implement effectively.

Another reason for impatience is the expectation that blockchain technology will solve all problems related to data security, privacy, and transparency. While blockchain technology is a powerful tool, it is not a panacea. There are still many challenges that need to be addressed, such as scalability, interoperability, and regulatory issues.

So, what can be done to address the issue of impatience in the blockchain space? The first step is to educate people about the technology and its potential. This means explaining the benefits and limitations of blockchain technology in a clear and concise manner. People need to understand that blockchain is not a magic solution that will solve all problems overnight, but rather a powerful tool that can be used to achieve specific goals.

Another important step is to manage expectations. Companies and organizations that are implementing blockchain technology need to be realistic about what they can achieve in the short term. This means setting achievable goals and milestones, and communicating those goals to stakeholders in a transparent manner.

It is also important to focus on the long-term potential of blockchain technology. While the technology is still in its early stages of development, there is no doubt that it has the potential to create significant change in many industries. By focusing on the long-term potential of blockchain, people can be motivated to continue investing in the technology, even when immediate results are not forthcoming.

Another way to address the issue of impatience is to focus on incremental improvements. Rather than trying to implement a fully functional blockchain solution all at once, companies and organizations can start by implementing smaller, more manageable solutions. This can help build momentum and generate interest in the technology, while also allowing for gradual improvements and adjustments.

Finally, it is important to remember that blockchain technology is not a one-size-fits-all solution. Different industries and use cases will require different implementations of blockchain technology. It is important to take the time to understand the specific needs of each industry and use case, and tailor blockchain solutions accordingly.

In conclusion, impatience is a common issue when it comes to emerging technologies like blockchain. While the potential of blockchain technology is undeniable, it is important to manage expectations and focus on the long-term potential of the technology. By educating people about the benefits and limitations of blockchain, managing expectations, focusing on incremental improvements, and tailoring solutions to specific use cases, we can help ensure that the potential of blockchain technology is fully realized in the years to come.

Being Impatient

Blockchain technology has been hailed as a game-changer in various industries, promising to bring about greater transparency, security, and efficiency. However, as with any new technology, there are challenges and limitations that need to be addressed before the full potential of blockchain can be realized. One common mistake that people make when it comes to blockchain is being impatient and expecting immediate results.

Being impatient can lead to unrealistic expectations and may cause individuals and organizations to give up on the technology prematurely. In this chapter, we will explore the consequences of being impatient in the context of blockchain technology and provide recommendations on how to approach the technology with a more realistic mindset.

The Consequences of Being Impatient

One of the biggest consequences of being impatient is the risk of overlooking the need for proper development and implementation of blockchain solutions. Blockchain is still a relatively new technology, and many of its applications are still in the experimental phase. Rushing to implement blockchain solutions without thoroughly testing them can result in serious consequences, such as vulnerabilities in the system, data breaches, and financial losses.

Another consequence of being impatient is the potential for missing out on the long-term benefits of blockchain technology. While blockchain has the potential to create significant change in many industries, it is important to remember that the benefits may not be immediate. For example, implementing a blockchain solution in the supply chain industry may take time to show its full potential in terms of reducing costs and improving efficiency. However, with patience and a long-term perspective, the benefits can be significant.

Finally, being impatient can lead to a lack of understanding of how blockchain works and its limitations. Blockchain technology is complex, and it requires a deep understanding of the underlying principles to fully appreciate its potential. Rushing into implementing blockchain solutions without a solid understanding of the technology can lead to mistakes, such as overestimating its capabilities or underestimating its limitations.

How to Approach Blockchain with a Realistic Mindset

To avoid the consequences of being impatient, it is important to approach blockchain technology with a realistic mindset. Here are some recommendations:

Educate yourself: The first step in approaching blockchain with a realistic mindset is to educate yourself about the technology. Learn how blockchain works, its limitations, and its potential applications in different industries. There are numerous resources available online, including whitepapers, research papers, and online courses.

Take a long-term perspective: Blockchain is a long-term investment, and it is important to take a long-term perspective when implementing blockchain solutions. Focus on the potential benefits that blockchain can provide in the future, rather than immediate results.

Collaborate with experts: Blockchain is a complex technology, and it is important to collaborate with experts who have experience in implementing blockchain solutions. Seek out partnerships with blockchain developers, consultants, and other experts who can provide guidance and support.

Test and iterate: Blockchain solutions should be thoroughly tested and iterated before implementation. Conduct extensive testing to identify potential vulnerabilities and bugs, and make necessary adjustments to ensure that the system is secure and functioning as intended.

Be patient: Finally, it is important to be patient when implementing blockchain solutions. Blockchain is still a new technology, and its full potential may not be realized for some time.

However, with patience and a realistic mindset, the benefits of blockchain can be significant.

Conclusion

Blockchain technology has the potential to create significant change in many industries, but it requires patience and a realistic mindset to fully realize its potential. Being impatient can lead to unrealistic expectations, overlooking the need for proper development and implementation, and missing out on the long-term benefits of the technology. By educating yourself, taking a long-term perspective, collaborating with experts, testing and iterating, and being patient, you can approach blockchain with a realistic mindset and unlock its full potential.

Not Limiting Access: The Risks of Unrestricted Access to Blockchain Data

Blockchain technology is often touted for its security and transparency, but it is not immune to security risks. One major risk that can compromise the security of blockchain data is unrestricted access. When access to blockchain data is not limited, anyone can access it, including cyber criminals, hackers, and even competitors.

In this chapter, we will explore the risks associated with not limiting access to blockchain data, as well as strategies for mitigating these risks.

The Risks of Unrestricted Access

Unrestricted access to blockchain data can lead to a range of security risks, including:

Unauthorized access: Without proper access controls, anyone can access blockchain data, including sensitive data such as financial transactions, personal information, and trade secrets. This can lead to theft, fraud, and other malicious activities.

Data tampering: Unrestricted access can also make it easier for attackers to tamper with blockchain data. For example, an attacker could change the outcome of a financial transaction or alter the ownership of a digital asset.

Insider threats: Unrestricted access can also create the risk of insider threats. Employees, contractors, or other insiders with access to blockchain data could use this access for personal gain or to harm the organization.

Regulatory compliance: Many industries are subject to regulations that require them to limit access to sensitive data. Failure to comply with these regulations can result in fines, legal action, and damage to the organization's reputation.

Strategies for Mitigating the Risks

To mitigate the risks associated with unrestricted access to blockchain data, organizations should consider implementing the following strategies:

Access controls: Access controls are a critical component of any security strategy. Organizations should implement access controls to limit access to sensitive blockchain data to only those who need it.

Encryption: Encryption can be used to protect blockchain data from unauthorized access. By encrypting blockchain data, even if an attacker gains access to it, they will not be able to read it without the encryption key.

Audit trails: Audit trails can be used to track who has accessed blockchain data and what changes have been made. This can help organizations identify unauthorized access and data tampering.

Compliance monitoring: Organizations subject to regulatory compliance should implement monitoring and reporting mechanisms to ensure they are meeting compliance requirements.

Employee training: Employee training is an essential component of any security strategy. Organizations should educate employees on the risks associated with unrestricted access to blockchain data and provide training on how to identify and report suspicious activity.

Conclusion

Unrestricted access to blockchain data can compromise the security of an organization's sensitive information and lead to a range of security risks. To mitigate these risks, organizations should implement access controls, encryption, audit trails, compliance monitoring, and employee training. By taking these steps, organizations can ensure that their blockchain data remains secure and protected from unauthorized access and data tampering.

Poor Planning

Poor Planning - The Risks of Rushing into Blockchain Implementation

Blockchain technology has the potential to revolutionize industries by increasing efficiency, transparency, and security. However, the implementation of blockchain is not always easy, and it requires careful planning and execution. Rushing into blockchain implementation without proper planning can lead to serious risks and challenges that could undermine the benefits of the technology. In this chapter, we will discuss the risks of poor planning when implementing blockchain technology and provide recommendations on how to avoid these risks.

Lack of clear objectives and use cases

One of the biggest risks of poor planning is the lack of clear objectives and use cases for blockchain technology. Blockchain is not a one-size-fits-all solution, and it is important to identify specific use cases that can benefit from blockchain technology. Without clear objectives and use cases, blockchain implementation can be inefficient, costly, and fail to deliver the expected benefits. Organizations must carefully evaluate the potential use cases and determine whether blockchain is the best solution for their specific needs.

Inadequate preparation and research

Another risk of poor planning is inadequate preparation and research. Blockchain technology is complex, and its implementation requires specialized knowledge and skills. Inadequate preparation and research can lead to technical challenges and security vulnerabilities, which could compromise the integrity of the blockchain network. Organizations must invest in adequate preparation and research to understand the technology and ensure that they have the necessary skills and expertise to implement and maintain the blockchain network.

Lack of stakeholder buy-in and participation

A lack of stakeholder buy-in and participation is another risk of poor planning. Blockchain implementation requires the participation of multiple stakeholders, including developers, users, and regulators. Without stakeholder buy-in and participation, blockchain implementation can be met with resistance and fail to achieve its goals. It is important to involve stakeholders from the beginning and communicate the benefits of blockchain technology to gain their support and participation.

Insufficient budget and resources

Blockchain implementation requires significant investment in terms of budget and resources. Poor planning can result in insufficient budget and resources, which can compromise the quality and effectiveness of the blockchain network. Organizations must carefully evaluate the costs and allocate sufficient resources to ensure that the blockchain network is properly implemented and maintained.

Lack of integration with existing systems

Another risk of poor planning is the lack of integration with existing systems. Blockchain implementation should not be seen as a standalone solution, but rather as part of a broader ecosystem. Failure to integrate blockchain with existing systems can lead to inefficiencies and redundancies, reducing the effectiveness of the blockchain network. It is important to plan for the integration of blockchain with existing systems from the beginning and ensure that the blockchain network is compatible with the organization's infrastructure.

Failure to comply with regulations and standards

Blockchain technology is subject to regulations and standards, and failure to comply with these regulations and standards can result in legal and reputational risks. Poor planning can result in a failure to comply with regulations and standards, which could compromise the integrity of the blockchain network and undermine its effectiveness. Organizations must carefully evaluate the regulatory and legal landscape and ensure that their blockchain implementation complies with all relevant regulations and standards.

Lack of contingency planning

Finally, poor planning can result in a lack of contingency planning. Blockchain implementation can be subject to unforeseen challenges and risks, and it is important to have a contingency plan in place to address these challenges. Failure to have a contingency plan in place can result in significant disruptions and compromise the effectiveness of the blockchain network. Organizations must plan for contingencies and have a clear roadmap for addressing challenges that may arise during blockchain implementation.

Conclusion:

Blockchain technology has the potential to create significant change in many industries, but its implementation requires careful planning and execution. Poor planning can lead to significant risks and challenges that could undermine the benefits of the technology. By carefully evaluating the potential risks and challenges of blockchain technology and developing a comprehensive plan for its implementation, organizations can avoid many of the pitfalls associated with this emerging technology.

Poor planning is one of the biggest obstacles to successful blockchain implementation. This can take many forms, including insufficient investment in infrastructure, lack of understanding of the technology, and unrealistic expectations. Without proper planning, organizations may find themselves struggling to adapt to the unique demands of blockchain technology, leading to missed opportunities and lost investments.

One common mistake in poor planning is underestimating the infrastructure required to support a blockchain network. Blockchain technology relies heavily on decentralized nodes to maintain its security and resilience. This means that significant resources are required to ensure that the network remains operational at all times. Without the proper infrastructure in place, organizations may find themselves unable to keep up with the demands of the network, leading to downtime, security breaches, and other issues.

Another common issue with poor planning is a lack of understanding of the technology. Blockchain is a complex and rapidly evolving technology that requires a high level of technical expertise to properly implement and manage. Many organizations may lack the necessary skills or resources to effectively leverage the benefits of blockchain technology, leading to missed opportunities and inefficient operations.

Finally, unrealistic expectations can also be a major obstacle to successful blockchain implementation. Blockchain technology is often touted as a silver bullet that can solve all of an organization's problems overnight. In reality, however, blockchain is just one tool among many that can help organizations achieve their goals. Failing to recognize the limitations of the technology and setting unrealistic expectations can lead to disappointment and a loss of faith in the technology.

To avoid the risks associated with poor planning, organizations must take a comprehensive approach to blockchain implementation. This involves a thorough assessment of the organization's needs and capabilities, as well as a clear understanding of the risks and challenges associated with the technology. Organizations must also invest in the necessary infrastructure and technical expertise to support the network, and develop realistic expectations for the role that blockchain technology will play in their operations.

One effective approach to blockchain implementation is to start small and build gradually. This allows organizations to test the technology in a controlled environment, identify potential issues, and refine their approach over time. It also allows organizations to demonstrate the value of blockchain technology to stakeholders, build support for the technology, and secure additional resources for further expansion.

Another key element of successful blockchain implementation is collaboration. Blockchain technology is inherently decentralized, meaning that it requires the cooperation of multiple parties to operate effectively. This means that organizations must work closely with partners and stakeholders to develop a shared vision for the use of blockchain technology, and to identify opportunities for collaboration and mutual benefit.

In conclusion, poor planning is a major obstacle to successful blockchain implementation. Organizations must take a comprehensive approach to blockchain implementation, investing in the necessary infrastructure and technical expertise, developing realistic expectations, and collaborating closely with partners and stakeholders. By taking these steps, organizations can overcome the challenges associated with blockchain technology and unlock the full potential of this powerful tool.

Lack of Clear Objectives

One of the biggest challenges that organizations face when implementing blockchain technology is the lack of clear objectives. Blockchain technology is not a silver bullet solution that can solve all problems. Therefore, it is essential to have a clear understanding of the objectives that the technology is meant to achieve.

Without clear objectives, organizations may struggle to determine the appropriate blockchain platform, the level of investment required, and the timeline for implementation. In this chapter, we will discuss the importance of having clear objectives when implementing blockchain technology and the risks associated with a lack of clear objectives.

The Importance of Clear Objectives

Clear objectives are essential when implementing blockchain technology. Blockchain technology can be used to solve a wide range of business problems, but it is essential to have a clear understanding of the problem that needs to be solved. The objectives of implementing blockchain technology should be aligned with the organization's overall strategy.

Clear objectives help to ensure that the organization is investing in the right blockchain platform. Different blockchain platforms have different strengths and weaknesses. Some blockchain platforms are better suited for specific use cases than others. Having clear objectives helps organizations to choose the blockchain platform that is best suited to their needs.

Clear objectives also help organizations to determine the level of investment required. Implementing blockchain technology can be expensive, and it is essential to determine the level of investment required to achieve the desired outcomes. Clear objectives help to ensure that the organization is investing the right amount of resources to achieve the desired outcomes.

Finally, clear objectives help organizations to determine the timeline for implementation. Blockchain technology implementation can be time-consuming, and having clear objectives helps organizations to determine how long it will take to achieve the desired outcomes.

Risks Associated with a Lack of Clear Objectives

A lack of clear objectives when implementing blockchain technology can lead to significant risks and challenges. The following are some of the risks associated with a lack of clear objectives.

Choosing the Wrong Platform

Choosing the wrong blockchain platform can lead to significant risks and challenges. Different blockchain platforms have different strengths and weaknesses, and some platforms are better suited for specific use cases than others. Without clear objectives, organizations may choose the wrong blockchain platform, which can lead to wasted resources, delays in implementation, and suboptimal outcomes.

Over or Under Investment

Implementing blockchain technology can be expensive, and a lack of clear objectives can lead to over or under investment. Without clear objectives, organizations may invest too much or too little in blockchain technology, which can lead to suboptimal outcomes.

Delayed Implementation

A lack of clear objectives can also lead to delayed implementation. Without clear objectives, organizations may struggle to determine the appropriate blockchain platform, the level of investment required, and the timeline for implementation. This can lead to delays in implementation and missed opportunities.

Failure to Achieve Desired Outcomes

Finally, a lack of clear objectives can lead to failure to achieve the desired outcomes. Without clear objectives, organizations may not fully understand the problem that needs to be solved or the desired outcomes. This can lead to suboptimal outcomes and failure to achieve the desired outcomes.

Conclusion

Clear objectives are essential when implementing blockchain technology. Clear objectives help organizations to choose the right blockchain platform, determine the level of investment required, and the timeline for implementation. A lack of clear objectives can lead to significant risks and challenges, including choosing the wrong platform, over or under investment, delayed implementation, and failure to achieve the desired outcomes. Organizations should take the time to carefully consider their objectives before implementing blockchain technology to ensure that they are investing their resources wisely and achieving the desired outcomes.

Failing to Build a Support Network

Blockchain technology is often viewed as a solution to a range of problems across various industries. While the technology holds a lot of potential, it can be challenging to implement and maintain effectively. One common mistake that organizations make when adopting blockchain technology is failing to build a support network.

A support network is crucial to the success of any blockchain project. This network should consist of a team of experts who understand the technology and can provide guidance on its implementation and use. These experts may include developers, cybersecurity specialists, legal advisors, and industry experts. Without a support network, organizations may struggle to address issues as they arise, and the project may fail.

The Importance of a Support Network

Implementing blockchain technology requires specialized knowledge and skills that may not be available in-house. A support network can provide access to this expertise and help organizations overcome any obstacles that arise during implementation. A support network can also provide guidance on best practices, such as security measures and regulatory compliance.

Additionally, a support network can provide a broader perspective on the use cases of blockchain technology. By engaging with experts in different industries, organizations can gain insights into how blockchain has been successfully implemented and the challenges that may arise. This can help organizations tailor their approach to their specific industry and achieve better results.

The Risks of Not Having a Support Network

The risks of not having a support network can be significant. Without a support network, organizations may struggle to identify potential risks and address them effectively. This can lead to security breaches, data loss, and other negative outcomes. Additionally, without a support network, organizations may not be able to optimize the use of blockchain technology, leading to wasted resources and missed opportunities.

Not having a support network can also result in a lack of understanding of the technology's potential. This can lead to unrealistic expectations and disappointment when the technology does not meet those expectations. This, in turn, can lead to a loss of faith in the technology and a reluctance to invest in its adoption in the future.

Building a Support Network

Building a support network requires a deliberate and strategic approach. The first step is to identify the expertise required for the specific blockchain project. This may include developers, cybersecurity specialists, legal advisors, industry experts, and other professionals. Once these experts have been identified, they should be engaged early in the planning process to provide guidance and input.

Networking events, conferences, and online forums can also be useful tools for building a support network. These events provide opportunities to engage with experts in the field and learn from their experiences. Organizations can also consider partnering with other organizations in their industry to build a support network together.

Maintaining a Support Network

Maintaining a support network is just as important as building one. Organizations should regularly engage with their support network to ensure that they remain up-to-date on best practices and developments in the field. This can involve regular meetings, training sessions, and updates on the progress of the blockchain project.

It is also important to regularly assess the effectiveness of the support network. Organizations should seek feedback from their support network and make any necessary changes to ensure that they are getting the most out of their network.

Conclusion

Failing to build a support network is a common mistake that organizations make when adopting blockchain technology. Without a support network, organizations may struggle to address issues as they arise, and the project may fail. Building a support network requires a deliberate and strategic approach, and maintaining the network is just as important as building it. By building a strong support network, organizations can access the expertise required to implement blockchain technology effectively and achieve better results.

Blockchain technology has the potential to revolutionize many industries by providing transparency, security, and accountability. However, its implementation requires careful planning and execution. One of the common mistakes made in implementing blockchain technology is failing to limit access to it. Failing to limit access to the blockchain can lead to various risks, including security breaches, malicious attacks, and manipulation of data. It is crucial to have a comprehensive access control strategy in place to ensure the security and integrity of the blockchain. By limiting access and implementing appropriate security measures, organizations can reap the benefits of blockchain technology without compromising their data security.

www.ingramcontent.com/pod-product-compliance
Lightning Source LLC
Chambersburg PA
CBHW041208220326
41597CB00030BA/5091